BERKLEE
CONTEMPORARY MUSIC THEORY

VESSELA STOYANOVA • JEFF PERRY

BERKLEE PRESS

Editor in Chief: Jonathan Feist

Senior Vice President of Pre-College, Online, and Professional Programs/
CEO and Cofounder of Berklee Online: Debbie Cavalier

RECORDING
Jesse Taitt, Piano
John Pierce, Engineer
All audio examples recorded at Stonewall Studio, Stoneham MA

ISBN 978-0-87639-230-0

Berklee
Press

1140 Boylston Street • MS-855BP
Boston, MA 02215-3693 USA

Visit Berklee Press Online at
www.berkleepress.com

Berklee Online

Study music online at
online.berklee.edu

DISTRIBUTED BY

HAL•LEONARD®

Visit Hal Leonard Online
www.halleonard.com

Berklee Press, a publishing activity of Berklee College of Music, is a not-for-profit educational publisher.
Available proceeds from the sales of our products are contributed to the scholarship funds of the college.

CONTENTS

Acknowledgments v

Preface vii

PART I. THE FOUNDATION 1

    Chapter 1. Basic Notation and Terms 2

    Chapter 2. Rhythm and Meter 6

    Chapter 3. Pitch, Notation, and the Keyboard 17

    Chapter 4. Intervals and Scales 24

    Chapter 5. Triads 35

    Chapter 6. Key Signatures; Circle of Fifths 38

    Chapter 7. Diatonic Harmony in Major Keys; Roman Numerals 42

    Chapter 8. Diatonic Harmony in Minor Keys 46

    Chapter 9. Major and Minor Key Diatonic Harmony in Seventh Chords;
            Harmonic Function 48

    Chapter 10. Tensions and Avoid Notes 54

    Chapter 11. Form Reading: Charts and Lead Sheets 58

    Chapter 12. The Role of the Rhythm Section 62

    Chapter 13. Blues Form, Progression, and Scale 70

PART II. CHROMATIC ALTERATIONS 75

    Chapter 14. Secondary Dominants and Related II Chords 76

    Chapter 15. Extended Dominants; Interpolated II Chords 85

    Chapter 16. Compound Minor Key Harmony Using Seventh Chords 88

    Chapter 17. Modal Interchange 92

    Chapter 18. Melodic Development: Approach Notes 95

    Chapter 19. Substitute Dominants and Related II Chords; Extended subV7s 97

    Chapter 20. Standard Deceptive Resolution of the Primary Dominant 104

    Chapter 21. Chord Scale Theory; Modes 107

    Chapter 22. Diminished Chords and Chord Scales 119

    Chapter 23. Modulation 126

    Chapter 24. Blues Reharmonization 131

    Chapter 25. Advanced Chord Voicings: Polychords; Hybrid Chords 134

    Chapter 26. Contiguous Dominants and Constant Structure 141

PART III. MODAL HARMONY 143

Chapter 27. Basic Signifiers of Modal Music 145

Chapter 28. Characteristic Pitch and Typical Cadences for Each of the Seven Modes 147

Chapter 29. Pedal Point and Ostinato 150

Index 152

About the Authors 159

ACKNOWLEDGMENTS

We owe a tremendous deal of gratitude to our colleagues, past and present, in the Harmony and Jazz Composition Department, and the Contemporary Writing and Production Department at Berklee, who are dedicated to building and preserving a legacy of elegant, flexible, and practical curriculum that allows better understanding of common use practices, while constantly evolving and expanding. We humbly stand on the shoulders of giants.

We would like to thank Berklee Summer Programs and Berklee Press for understanding the need for this book and supporting us in the effort of publishing it. A special thanks to our editor in chief Jonathan Feist for his uncanny ability to catch and dispel any lack of clarity, redundancy, or inconsistency with apparent ease that at times seemed beyond human.

Finally, and most importantly, we are forever grateful to the creators of Aspire: Five-Week Summer Performance Intensive, Rob Rose and Bob Doezema. We are both very fortunate to work with our current director John Pierce, who creates a work environment more akin to a loving family than a sterile office—a place where we feel supported and respected even if we disagree on the specifics, a place that is conducive to creativity, innovation, and inspiration, while always keeping high standards for ourselves, our faculty and our students.

We can say without a doubt that this program is life changing. Not only have we witnessed it with many of our students but we have both experienced it first hand in the role it has played in our lives.

PREFACE

There are many benefits to understanding music theory. When used appropriately, it provides an invaluable set of tools for any musician, regardless of instrument, style, age, or level of proficiency. From the very basic terms to more sophisticated concepts and ideas, music theory serves as a common language among musicians. It helps us communicate with each other during rehearsals, enhances our memory for new repertoire, opens the curtains, and reveals the thought processes of composers and performers that came before us.

One of the main reasons musicians study music theory is to develop a skill that translates what one hears into written form, and conversely, interpret written music into sound. In other words: the ability to *see what you hear and hear what you see.*

As with any new language, we need to learn the alphabet, build a vocabulary of useful words and phrases, learn the rules of grammar, and seamlessly over time begin using it to express ideas, emotions, descriptions, jokes, abstractions, and beyond. Learning music theory is an exciting and fulfilling endeavor that we hope this book will make enjoyable as well.

HOW TO BEST USE THIS BOOK

The material covered in this book has an internal logic of chronology and is well suited for the perfect beginner. However, a more advanced student may begin at any chapter of interest and jump around as desired. Although its use as a textbook for the Aspire: Five-Week Music Performance Intensive assumes the guidance of a teacher, it is perfectly accessible for self-study as well.

Each chapter succinctly covers the concept and offers audio examples. The drill corner provides specific recommendations for memorization of material, and when appropriate, we suggest instrumental practicing. Vocalists, drummers, and non-chordal instrumentalists are encouraged to play select musical examples on piano.

 An online *Assignments* booklet will help you reinforce each lesson's concepts, as indicated throughout by this icon.

Go to www.halleonard.com/mylibrary to download the *Assignments* booklet and its associated answer key, entering the access code found on the first page of this book.

We strongly recommend that you listen and play the musical examples and repeat them as many times as needed before continuing with the reading. This book is not meant as a cerebral exercise, but rather an immersive musical one. To that end, we provide real-life musical examples that demonstrate the concepts we discuss. We recommend that you find these concepts in the music you play or listen to.

One final word of advice: build a vast repertoire of pieces you can play by memory; listen to a wide array of genres, styles, and artists; keep an open mind; and collaborate with other musicians whenever possible. The power of music comes from its ability to create human connection that defies time, space, and prejudice, as we all strive together to be its worthy ambassadors.

About the Audio

To access the accompanying audio, go to www.halleonard.com/mylibrary and enter the code found on the first page of this book. This will grant you instant access to every example. Examples with accompanying audio are marked with an audio icon.

Part I

The Foundation

CHAPTER 1

Basic Notation and Terms

The first step on this lifelong journey begins with a few terms we need to be familiar with and learn to use correctly.

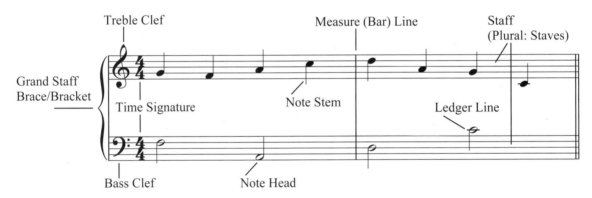

FIG. 1.1. Basic Notation Terms

Here is a brief explanation of each element depicted in figure 1.1. Later on, we will introduce many more elements, as well as elaborate further on some of these.

staff (plural: **staves**)	The five lines and four spaces we use to position notes; each line and space represents a consecutive pitch.
grand staff	Two single staves joined by a "brace" (bracket) that indicates that the two staves are played simultaneously by the same person, and on the same instrument.
note head	The part of the note that is positioned on a line or space on the staff. It represents a specific pitch, based on the clef at the beginning of the staff.
note stem	The vertical line (or handle) of the note. If the note head is above the middle line of the staff, the stem extends down; if the note head is below the middle line, the stem extends up. If the note head is on the middle line, the stem may go up or down. Stems are usually the length of an octave worth of staff space except in special cases.

ledger line	An extension to the five-line staff added to accommodate pitches that go beyond the five lines and four spaces. Regular notation typically uses up to three ledger lines. They are spaced the same distance from each other as the lines of the staff.
clef	The symbol at the beginning of the staff that indicates which pitches are represented on the staff.
treble clef	Assigns the note G4 (the G above middle C) to the second line from the bottom and orients the rest of the notes accordingly. It is generally used by instruments in the middle to high range of pitch.
bass clef	Assigns the note F3 (the F below middle C) to the fourth line from the bottom. It is generally used by instruments with low pitch.
measure line (aka **barline**)	Separates the music into measures (bars) in order to provide a visual aid in following or reading the music.

Notice the exact relationship between the note head and the stem. If the stem goes down, the note head is to its right; if the stem goes up, the note head is to its left.

FIG. 1.2. Stem Direction and Length

The shape of the note or rest indicates its duration as follows.

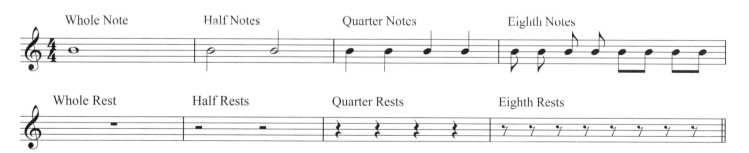

FIG. 1.3. Note and Rest Durations

DRILL CORNER

Memorize the terms discussed in this chapter so far!

 ASSIGNMENT 1.1

ADDITIONAL NOTATION TERMS

Here are a few more useful terms that you need to be familiar with. Feel free to come back to this page as often as you need to.

accidental	A sharp, flat, or natural sign that alters the pitch of a note in addition to the key signature indicated in the beginning of the staff.
key signature	A collection of sharps or flats that indicates which of the pitches are played a half step higher or a half step lower from their letter name. The key signature establishes a tonal center and a hierarchy of pitches. We will come back to this in much more detail later.
time signature	Positioned after the key signature on the staff, it indicates how many beats and of what value appear in each measure. More on this in the chapter on rhythm.
tempo marking	Positioned above the staff, it may appear as a number or a word, usually in Italian or English. The number indicates beats per minute and is a lot more accurate than the word, which implies a range of similar tempos.
double barline	Indicates the end of a section.
final barline	Indicates the end of the piece.
beam	The horizontal or slanted line that connects two or more eighth notes.
note flag	A symbol attached to the stem of the note turning a quarter note into an eighth note.

Notice that the flag always appears to the right of the stem, regardless of which direction the stem extends.

FIG. 1.4. Additional Notation Terms

flat (♭)	Lowers the pitch by a half step.
sharp (♯)	Raises the pitch by a half step.
double flat (♭♭)	Lowers the pitch by a whole step.
double sharp (✗)	Raises the pitch by a whole step.
natural (♮)	Cancels the existing key signature or accidental earlier in the measure. In that sense, it may lower or raise the pitch of the note depending on whether it is canceling a sharp or a flat. A single natural sign will cancel a double flat or sharp. There is no such thing as a double natural sign.

FIG. 1.5. Accidentals

ACCIDENTALS

- All accidentals are written to the left of the note head regardless of stem direction.

- They occupy the same space or line as the note head they are intended for. In the case of a complex chord with many accidentals, they may be far away from the note heads, which makes it even more important to position them correctly.

- An accidental applies to all the following notes of the same pitch within a measure. A note with the same name in a different octave is not affected by the accidental.

- A single natural sign cancels double sharps or double flats; there is no such thing as a double natural sign.

- A courtesy accidental may be used as a reminder that a note is no longer affected by a previous accidental, usually because the note in question is in a new measure. Courtesy accidentals might be placed in parentheses.

 ASSIGNMENT 1.2

CHAPTER 2

Rhythm and Meter

Rhythm is the most basic element of music, closely followed by pitch. It refers to the pattern of sounds over a period of time. Written music uses differently shaped notes and rests to represent the different duration of sounds that create the rhythmic pattern.

Meter is an unsung hero of music. It is the inaudible organization of time into beats and measures. Meter gives contextual meaning to the notes and rests we use when notating duration. In written music, meter is indicated by time signatures, which consist of an upper number, usually showing how many beats are in each measure, and a lower number, indicating the duration of each beat.

A time signature of 4/4, for example, shows that each measure consists of four quarter notes, while a 3/2 time signature represents three half notes per measure.

- *Beats* **represent the underlying pulse of music.** They are often (but not always) represented by the lower number of the time signature.

- *Tempo* **refers to the absolute duration of each beat.** It is indicated by a number that represents beats per minute (bpm). For example ♩ = 60 means that each quarter note is one second (that is, 1/60 of a minute) long. Historically, composers have used descriptive words (often in Italian) such as vivo, allegro, lento—to indicate an acceptable range of bpm. These words often refer to the mood of the piece as well as the tempo and are not as accurate as a bpm indication. In contemporary practice, composers use their native language to describe the desired tempo, often accompanied by a specific bpm.

A musician needs to understand and master the elements described in order to be able to notate and/or read rhythms accurately. We'll explore each element throughout this book.

Let's start with the rhythmic values of notes and rests and their subdivisions, ranging from a whole note to sixteenth notes.

- A *whole note* or rest is worth four beats. It can be subdivided into two half notes or half rests, each worth two beats.
- A *half note* or rest can be subdivided into two quarter notes or rests, each worth a beat.
- A *quarter note* or rest can be subdivided into two eighth notes or rests, each worth half a beat.
- An *eighth note* or rest can be subdivided into two sixteenth notes or rests, each worth a quarter of a beat.

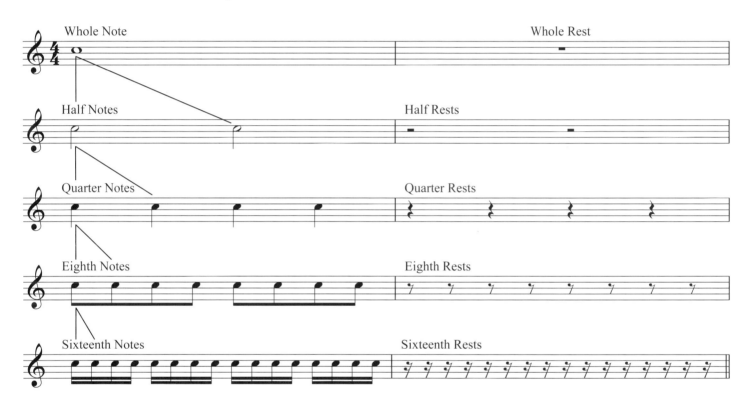

FIG. 2.1. Subdivision of Beats Represented by Notes and Rests in 4/4 Time

WHOLE REST POSITION

There is a convention in music notation to use a whole rest whenever the entire measure is silent, regardless of time signature. Notice the exact position of the whole measure rest: in the middle of the measure, "hanging from the ceiling" in the third space (see figure 2.1). By contrast, the whole note is always worth four beats, and it is positioned immediately after the barline.

Figure 2.1 shows the exact correspondence in duration between the different notes: a whole note is worth two half notes; a half note is worth two quarter notes; a quarter note is worth two eighth notes, and an eighth note is worth two sixteenth notes.

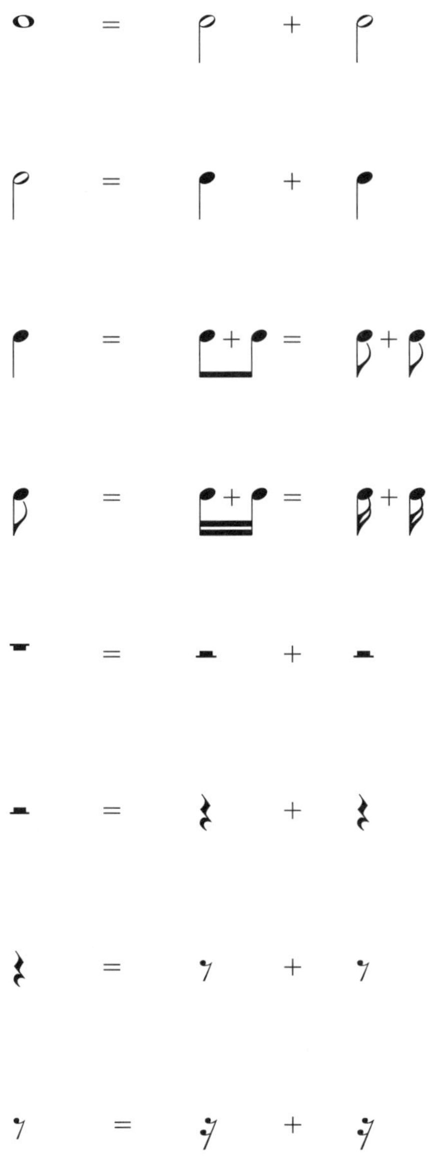

$$\mathbf{o} \quad = \quad \rho \quad + \quad \rho$$

$$\rho \quad = \quad \rho \quad + \quad \rho$$

$$\rho \quad = \quad \overset{}{\rho + \rho} = \beta + \beta$$

$$\beta \quad = \quad \overset{}{\rho + \rho} = \beta + \beta$$

$$\rule[0.5ex]{1em}{0.4pt} \quad = \quad \rule[0.2ex]{0.6em}{0.4pt} \quad + \quad \rule[0.2ex]{0.6em}{0.4pt}$$

$$\rule[0.2ex]{0.6em}{0.4pt} \quad = \quad \xi \quad + \quad \xi$$

$$\xi \quad = \quad \gamma \quad + \quad \gamma$$

$$\gamma \quad = \quad \gamma \quad + \quad \gamma$$

FIG. 2.2. Rhythmic Values

When eighth and sixteenth notes are grouped together as in figure 2.1, they are connected by a beam. When they appear singly, they require a flag—single for eighth notes, double for sixteenths.

FIG. 2.3. Eighth and Sixteenth Notes

Notice the direction of the stem and the side the flag is written on.

 ASSIGNMENT 2.1

DOTTED NOTES AND TIES

Next, we can add a dot to the right of each note or rest. A dot (.) adds half the value of the note or rest it is attached to.

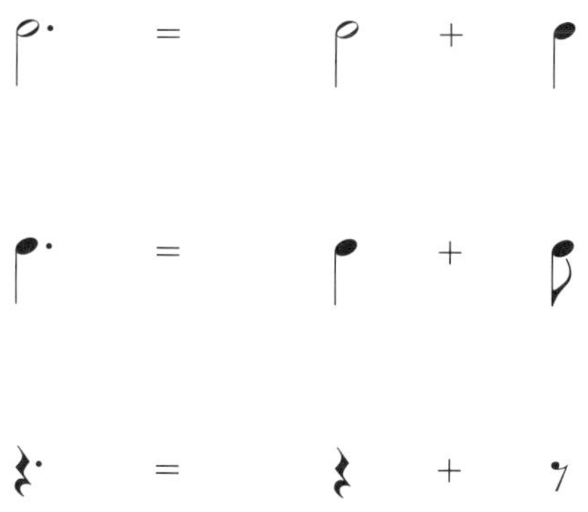

FIG. 2.4. Dotted Notes and Rests

Adding a *tie* between two notes combines their duration into one sound. Ties are most often used when the duration of a note crosses a barline.

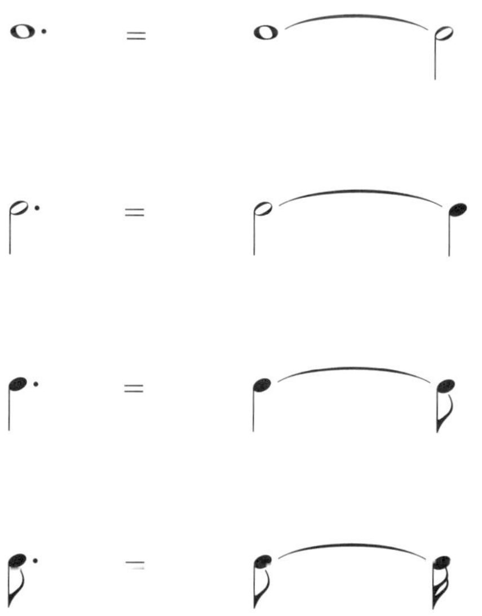

FIG. 2.5. Ties vs. Dotted Notes

Every meter contains an implied hierarchy of power between each beat. In a 4/4 meter, beat number 1 is strongest—meaning it has an implied heavier accent—followed by beat number 3, while beats 2 and 4 receive a weaker accent.

FIG. 2.6. Strong, Less Strong, and Weak Beats in 4/4

A time signature of 2/4 has a similar structure of emphasis: beat 1 is strong, while beat 2 is weak.

FIG. 2.7. Beat Emphasis in 4/4 and 2/4

In a triple meter, such as a time signature of 3/4, we see a collection of three beats per measure with beat 1 being strong, while beats 2 and 3 are weak.

FIG. 2.8. Beat Emphasis in 3/4

Reading rhythms may seem overwhelming at first, but over time, you can develop the ability to recognize rhythmic patterns that form recognizable phrases, much like a sentence is formed by a collection of words. Figure 2.9 shows all the possible patterns that comprise two beats, when using half, quarter, and eighth notes only.

FIG. 2.9. Two-Beat Patterns

As you can see, the list is not very long and quite manageable to memorize. Of course, each note can be replaced by a rest, which will add more variety to the combinations discussed.

DRILL CORNER

Memorize the eight two-beat rhythmic patterns from figure 2.9! The same exact patterns may be used to represent one beat, using sixteenth notes:

FIG. 2.10. Rhythmic Patterns Representing One Beat

NOTE DURATIONS AND HORIZONTAL SPACING

Notice that longer duration notes require more space than shorter duration ones. This is not an accident. Rhythmic notation uses an invisible grid that assigns a proportional amount of physical space that corresponds to the duration of the note.

FIG. 2.11. Rhythmic Grid

SKILL DEVELOPMENT

Sing, clap, and play on your instrument through the patterns in figure 2.9. Once you feel comfortable, jump around to a different pattern at will, creating different *sentences* by using the same *words*.

 ASSIGNMENT 2.2–2.3

IMAGINARY BARLINES

Another useful concept that helps with rhythmic pattern recognition is the *imaginary barline*. While the "real" barline visually divides time into measures in order to facilitate keeping track of music as it flows by, the imaginary barline further divides each measure into smaller parts. It is important to remember that the imaginary barline is not a visible symbol on the page, but rather a way to organize the rhythmic material into familiar patterns.

In a time signature of 4/4, when the smallest note subdivision is the eighth note, the imaginary barline divides the measure into two halves. If the smallest note subdivision is the sixteenth note, then the imaginary barline separates each beat, dividing the measure into four equal parts. Finally, if the smallest subdivision is the quarter note, there is no need for the imaginary barline.

Here are some examples of ignoring vs. observing the imaginary barline:

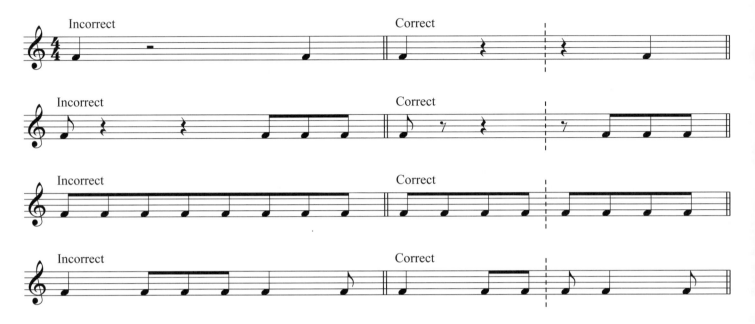

FIG. 2.12. Imaginary Barline

As you can see from figure 2.12, the imaginary barline cannot be crossed by a beam, much like a real barline. Notice that the correct notation results in using the familiar rhythmic patterns you memorized earlier in this chapter. One way of observing the imaginary barline rule is to imagine that you are rewriting the music that was written in 4/4 to a time signature of 2/4.

FIG. 2.13. Imaginary Barlines: Imagining 4/4 as 2/4

Another useful way to think about it is making sure that beat number 3 is visible.

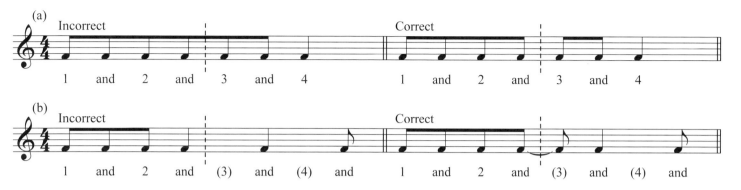

FIG. 2.14. Imaginary Barlines: Beat 3 Visible

In figure 2.14b, beat 3 is inside the quarter note, which is to say, the quarter note is crossing the imaginary barline. In order to fix the notation, we need to split the quarter note into two tied eighth notes, thus creating an object (the second eighth note) that is tied to beat 3. It is very important to then tie the two eighth notes, in order to maintain the original sound of the music. Remember, the imaginary barline concept is there to change what music looks like, not what it sounds like!

There are exceptions to the imaginary barline. The simplest way to think of the exception is "a half note or greater that occurs *on* the beat." Here are a few examples:

FIG. 2.15. Exceptions to Imaginary Barline

IMAGINARY BARLINE VARIATIONS

There are examples of notated music, usually influenced by certain folk traditions such as Latin, Balkan, or African, where the imaginary barline does not divide the measure into equal parts. Instead, it underlines the implied groove, which is often irregular. For example a measure of 4/4 may be divided into a dotted quarter, quarter, dotted quarter. In this case the imaginary barline will divide the measure into three parts: long, short, long.

When the rhythm requires the use of sixteenth notes, the imaginary barline appears between every beat. A convenient way to think about it is, each number should be visible:

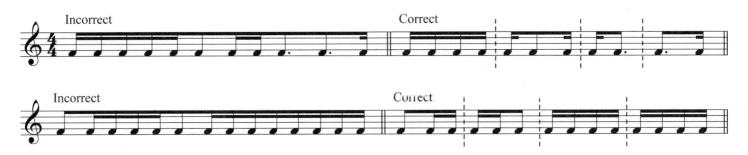

FIG. 2.16. Imaginary Barlines: Sixteenths

In 2/4 and 3/4 meters, we usually show each beat.

FIG. 2.17. Imaginary Barlines in 3/4 and 2/4

 ASSIGNMENT 2.4–2.5

COMPOUND METERS

So far, we have looked at *simple meters* such as 4/4, 3/4, and 2/4, where each beat can be subdivided into eighth notes or sixteenth notes. Here the beat or pulse is divisible by 2 (eighth notes) and 4 (sixteenth notes). When counting aloud, we use the syllables *1 and, 2 and...* for eighth notes and *1 ee and a, 2 ee and a...* for sixteenth notes.

FIG. 2.18. Counting Eighth and Sixteenth Notes

Another common way to divide the beat or pulse is by 3, using the syllables *1 and a, 2 and a...*, when counting. These are called *compound meters*, when the beat is divided into three subdivisions, rather than two. The two most common compound meters are 6/8 and 12/8.

One notable peculiarity of compound meters is the fact that the lower number of the time signature no longer represents the duration of the beat, but rather that of the subdivision. A 6/8 meter, although containing six eighth notes, has only two beats—each worth three eighth notes (or a dotted quarter note).

FIG. 2.19. Time Signature of 6/8

Similarly, a time signature of 12/8 represents a meter with four beats, each worth a dotted quarter note (three eighth notes).

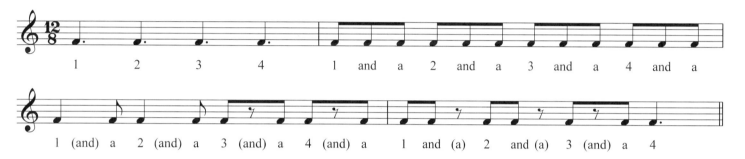

FIG. 2.20. Time Signature of 12/8

And just like we did in simple meters, we can imagine a barline that divides each beat of the compound meter as follows:

FIG. 2.21. Imaginary Barline in Compound Meters

It is impossible to address all the rhythmical possibilities that music will present in the course of your musical career, but it is important to address one more common occurrence: the triplet.

A triplet is used when the desired rhythm calls for a subdivision of a simple duple beat into three instead of two or four subdivisions. Triplets are widely used when only a few beats in a measure require a triple subdivision, while some remain subdivided in two.

1 2 and 3 and a 4 e and a

FIG. 2.22. Triplet

If all beats are subdivided in three, a compound meter may be more appropriate to use.

1 and a 2 and a 3 and a 4 and a

1 and a 2 and a 3 and a 4 and a

FIG. 2.23. Appropriate Use of a 12/8 Instead of 4/4

ASSIGNMENT 2.6

CHAPTER 3

Pitch, Notation, and the Keyboard

Pitch is indisputably one of the most important elements of music. From a scientific standpoint, pitch is described as the frequency of a sound wave through air per second. Frequency is measured in Hertz, abbreviated as Hz. The sound you hear when an American symphony orchestra is tuning before a performance is usually a frequency of 440 Hz. Using large numbers like that in a musical setting would be impractical, so musicians have adopted a simpler more practical method, naming pitch after the first seven letters of the alphabet—A, B, C, D, E, F, G—and attaching a number to each letter to indicate where in the range of hearing this pitch occurs. For example, the frequency of 440 Hz is recognized as A4, or the A above middle C on the piano.

FREQUENCY VS. PITCH

While frequency (Hz) is measured in absolute terms, pitch (note names) may have slight variations from culture to culture, era to era, instrument to instrument.

The human ear is capable of hearing a wide range of frequencies, although that varies from person to person, and often changes throughout one's life. The accuracy of pitch perception also varies greatly among individuals, and even among cultures. One thing is certain however, pitch recognition and reproduction is a trainable skill and a very important one.

Notating pitch has been a challenge for many generations of musicians. Today, we are able to do so fairly accurately with the aid of the five line stave, various clefs, and accidentals—flats, sharps, and natural signs. The two most commonly used clefs in contemporary notation are treble and bass, also known as G clef and F clef, respectively. Generally speaking, if an instrument or voice has a pitch range above G3 (the G below middle C), it uses treble clef.

FIG. 3.1. Treble Clef Melody

If an instrument or voice has a range lower than G3, it usually uses bass clef.

FIG. 3.2. Bass Clef Melody

In the case of the piano, which spans a range of pitches far too broad to fit in one clef, we use a grand staff—a combination of both treble and bass clef.

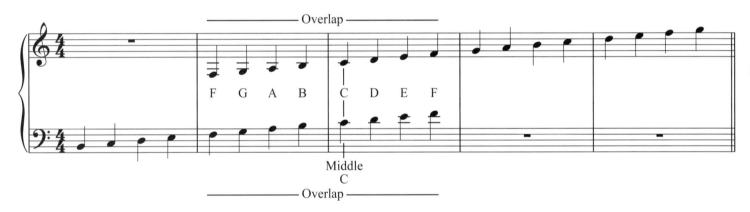

FIG. 3.3. Treble and Bass Clef Melody

It is important to be able to recognize written notes in both clefs immediately, rather than counting lines and spaces. This skill takes time and practice, but honing it delivers an invaluable tool of communication with other musicians and access to a wide range of repertoire.

Although there are many successful musicians who never learned to read and write music, not one of them would consider that an advantage.

 ASSIGNMENT 3.1

DRILL CORNER

Practice saying the note names of all notes in treble and bass clef, while pointing to their position on the staff. Experiment with going up and down, lines only, spaces only. Include ledger lines.

Pick any sheet music you have, and practice saying all of the note names. Put a metronome on and say the name of each note in time, starting slowly and gradually speeding up. Finally, say the note names following the rhythm of the piece.

Now that you are familiar with the names and positions of the notes in both treble and bass clefs, we are ready for the most important step—finding the written note on your instrument and/or the piano, and conversely, writing down on the staff a note you played. Remember, learn to *see what you hear and hear what you see.*

PIANO KEYBOARD

The layout of the piano is a tremendously useful tool when learning music theory. We will come back to it often, so it's a good idea to take some time and familiarize yourself with it, whether you play the piano or not.

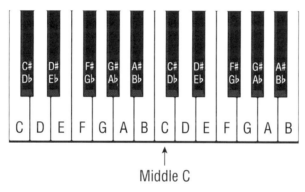

Middle C

FIG. 3.4. Keyboard

Important facts about the notes of the piano:
- The note names follow the English alphabet from A to G, then they repeat again.
- When there is a black key between the two white keys, the distance between white keys is a whole step.
- There are no black keys between the notes B and C, and the notes E and F. The distance between two white keys with no black key between them is a half step.
- Each black key has two possible names—one with a sharp and one with a flat. That is called *enharmonic spellings* (two different ways to spell the same pitch).
- The distance between a white key and the black key next to it is a half step.

Here is how the notated pitches map onto the white keys of the piano keyboard:

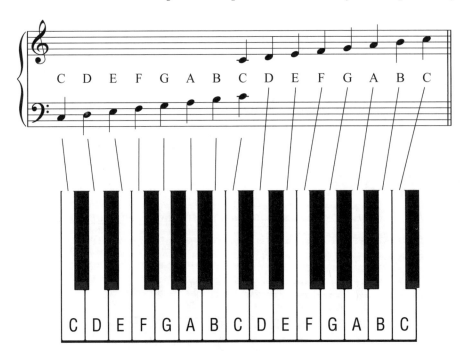

FIG. 3.5. Piano Keyboard to Staff Position Connection

Notice that middle C is shared by both the treble and the bass clef. A few notes on each side may be written in either clef using additional ledger lines. Musicians will often refer to pitch being lower or higher, which refers to the sound, or being to the left or to the right, which refers to the position on the keyboard. When looking at a piano, find middle C (or C4), and try to visualize treble clef to the right and bass clef to the left.

We use ledger lines to extend each staff beyond the five lines to capture the notes that fall outside the staff. It is impractical to use more than three ledger lines. If the music extends even further up or down, we typically use an *octava* sign. Abbreviated as *8va* when the music sounds an octave higher than written, and *8vb* when the music sounds an octave lower than written, the octava sign facilitates reading passages in the extreme range of the instrument. A dotted line indicates the length of the passage affected by the octave displacement.

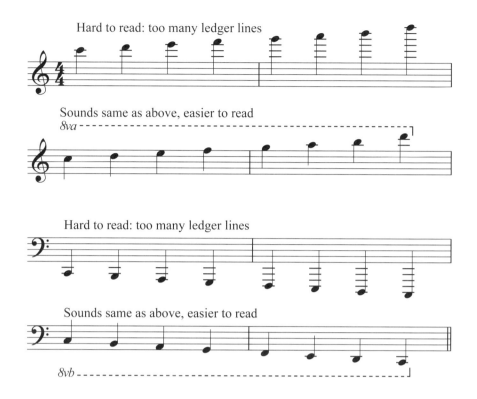

FIG. 3.6. Ledger Lines vs. 8va and 8vb Sign

We can use accidentals to capture the black keys. A sharp (♯) will raise the pitch by one half step and a flat (♭) will lower it by one half step.

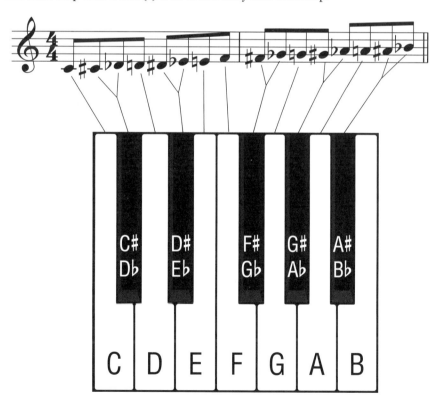

FIG. 3.7. Mapping Enharmonically Spelled Notes to the Keyboard

When a sharp or a flat is applied to a note, it remains in effect for that pitch for the duration of the measure. If we need to restore the original note, we use a natural sign (♮). The natural sign cancels any sharp or flat attached to the pitch in question, effectively either lowering or raising the pitch.

FIG. 3.8. Accidentals Change the Pitch by One Half Step

On rare occasions, usually for theoretical reasons, we need to use a double sharp (𝄪), which raises a pitch by a whole step, or a double flat (♭♭), which lowers the pitch by a whole step. A single natural sign will cancel either.

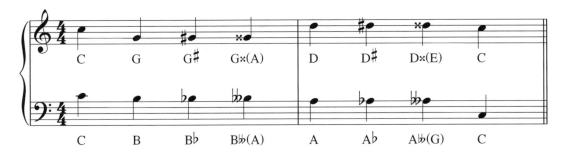

FIG. 3.9. Accidentals

When the key of a piece dictates that the same pitch or pitches should be consistently sharp or flat, we use a key signature. You can think of a key signature as a shortcut to avoid having to write the same accidental every time the note in question appears. We will look into key signatures in detail later in this book.

DRILL CORNER

1. Practice playing random notes on a keyboard and saying each note as you play.

2. Find written notes on your instrument (drummers and vocalists, use the piano!).

BEAMING GROUPS

As you recall from the chapter on rhythm, when multiple eighth or sixteenth notes happen in a row, we beam them together in groups. In the chapter on notation, we discussed the length and direction of each stem. Trying to follow the rules for both stem direction and beaming may present a challenge—how do we beam notes if their stems are supposed to go in different directions? The solution is negotiating a mutually acceptable arrangement: the note furthest from the middle line will typically determine the stem direction for all the notes in the beamed group. However, that may be overturned if the majority of notes are located on the opposite side of the middle line.

FIG. 3.10. Beaming Groups

 ASSIGNMENT 3.2–3.6

CHAPTER 4

Intervals and Scales

An *interval* is the distance between two pitches. When the two pitches are strung together sequentially, they create melody, and therefore the intervals between them are called *melodic intervals*. When the two pitches are stacked vertically, they create harmony, and the intervals between them are called *harmonic intervals*.

Western music has adopted a tuning system called *twelve tone equal temperament*, in which each octave (the distance between two pitches of the same name) is divided in twelve equal parts. Each part is called a semitone or half step, and it follows the rules of simple math: two half steps create a whole step, four half steps create two whole steps, etc.

You can hear the sound of the twelve consecutive half steps by playing every note on the piano, including the black notes between say middle C and the C an octave above. On the guitar, you can achieve the same by playing each adjacent fret on the same string.

We call that the *chromatic scale*. Since the half step (or semitone) is typically the smallest interval, we use that as a unit to measure the distance between two notes. For example, there are four semitones between the notes C and E (look at any keyboard or guitar fretboard, and you can verify that for yourself). However, referring to intervals by the number of semitones they encompass is impractical. Musicians have adopted a simple and practical method of categorizing and naming intervals by *quantity* and *quality*.

Quantity is expressed by ordinal numbers, such as second, third, fourth and so on, which refers to the number of letters involved in an interval. For example, the distance from C to E has the quantity of a third, since there are three letters involved: C, D, and E. You can also confirm the quantity of an interval by counting lines and spaces on the staff between the two notes.

The *quality* of an interval is expressed by an adjective such as major, minor, perfect, augmented, and diminished. It further refines the exact size of the interval, and is determined by the exact number of semitones involved.

Being able to hear, name, and construct intervals quickly and accurately is a crucial skill for any musician.

INTERVALS AND THE STAFF

Notice that counting lines and spaces on a staff does not confirm the quality of an interval, since the staff does not differentiate between half steps and whole steps! A close familiarity with the piano keyboard facilitates quality recognition greatly.

All intervals are divided into two categories, based on quality. Seconds, thirds, sixths, and sevenths come in four sizes (or qualities): major, minor, augmented, and diminished. Fourths, fifths, and octaves only come in three sizes: perfect, augmented, and diminished. The difference between each quality and the next is always a semitone or half step.

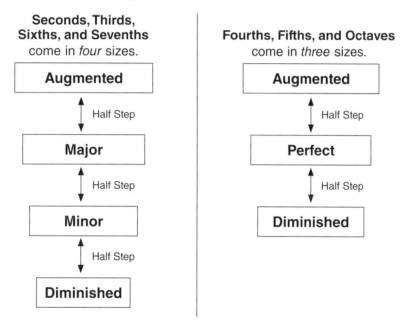

FIG. 4.1. Interval Sizes

Notice that the augmented fourth and the diminished fifth are the same size: three whole steps. This interval plays a crucial role in contemporary harmony and is often referred to as a *tritone*.

Here is a breakdown of the quantity and quality of the basic intervals up to an octave:

Interval Name	Abbreviation	Letters	Semitones Apart
unison	P1	1	0 (2 of the same note)
minor second	min2	2	1
major second	Maj2	2	2
minor third	min3	3	3
major third	Maj3	3	4 (2 whole steps)
perfect fourth	P4	4	5
augmented fourth	A4	4	6 (3 whole steps)
diminished fifth	D5	5	6 (3 whole steps)
perfect fifth	P5	5	7
minor sixth	min6	6	8 (4 whole steps)
major sixth	Maj6	6	9
minor seventh	min7	7	10 (5 whole steps)
major seventh	Maj7	7	11
perfect octave	P8	8	12 (6 whole steps)

Although it is good to know how many semitones are contained in each interval, at Berklee, we do not usually reference the number of semitones when determining the size of an interval larger than a minor third.

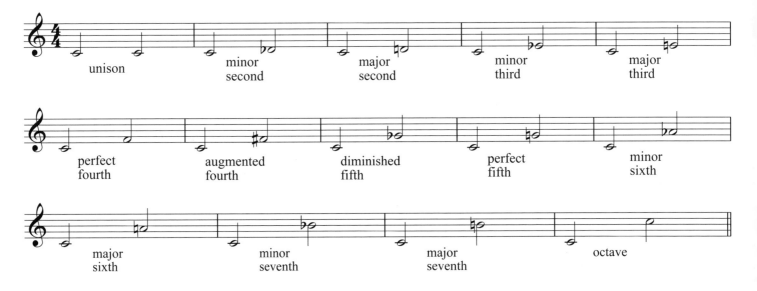

FIG. 4.2. Intervals

By now, you have probably realized that determining the quantity of an interval is fairly simple, while the quality may present a challenge. As mentioned, counting semitones is slow and impractical. In order to introduce a more practical approach, we must first be acquainted with the major and minor scales, which will provide a much-needed shortcut in interval identification.

INTRODUCTION TO SCALES

A *scale* is a sequence of notes that span an octave. The intervals between the notes of a scale may be half steps, whole steps, and sometimes a minor third. Most scales contain seven (of the twelve available) notes, although some contain as few as five and as many as eight. And of course, you are already familiar with the chromatic scale, which contains all twelve notes!

The *major scale* contains seven notes with a distinct ascending intervallic pattern: whole step, whole step, half step, whole step, whole step, whole step, half step. When starting on the note C, this intervallic pattern can easily be observed on a piano keyboard.

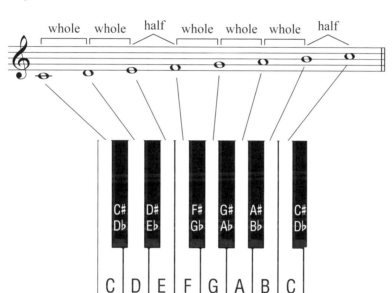

FIG. 4.3. C Major Scale and Piano Keyboard

Each note of the scale is called a *scale degree*. We use Arabic numbers to label the scale degrees of a major scale. We use solfège to sing each scale degree.

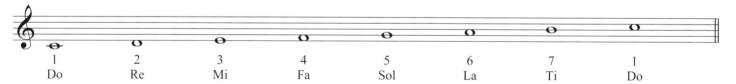

FIG. 4.4. Scale with Solfège

If we start on any note other than C, we will need to use black keys (and therefore accidentals) to maintain the intervallic relationship of the major scale.

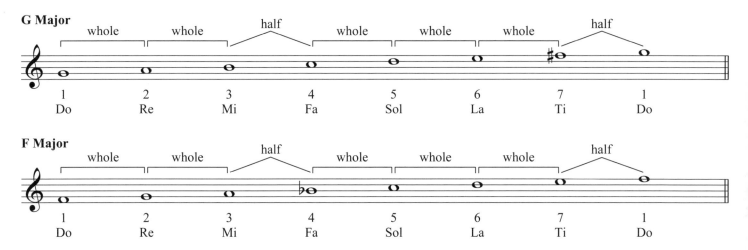

FIG. 4.5. G and F Major Scales

You can create a major scale starting on any of the twelve notes. Each starting note will require different accidentals in order to maintain the intervallic structure of the major scale. Since the same accidentals will be required every single time a note appears, musicians have invented a shortcut—the key signature. We will explore that concept and look at all the possible keys and their organization in the next chapter.

DRILL CORNER

Sing up and down the major scale using solfège, numbers, and letters. Switch between them half way through. Notice that when you change to a different major scale, only the letter names change. The numbers and solfège syllables remain the same.

Listen to "Music Box" by Regina Spektor to hear a full descending major scale in the opening line of the song.*

TONE TENDENCIES

As you sing through the major scale, notice how some scale degrees feel more stable than others. Do, Mi, and Sol feel stable, while Re has a tendency to move down to Do, Fa has a tendency to slide down to Mi, La has a tendency to slide down to Sol, Ti has a tendency to slide up to Do, and finally, Sol has a tendency to jump back up to Do. These organic tendencies lie in the foundation of the harmonic function theory, which we will examine later. For now, simply sing through the following sequence of scale degrees and feel the natural gravity of each scale degree.

---

* "Music Box" by Regina Spektor, *Begin to Hope (Deluxe Edition)*, Sire 9362-44112-2, 2006.

Pay extra attention to the pull between Ti and Do. This tendency is so powerful that it deserves its own name: Ti is also called a *leading tone*, as it leads our ear towards the stable Do.

2

Re   Do   Fa   Mi   La   Sol   Ti   Do   Sol   Do

FIG. 4.6. Tone Tendencies

NATURAL MINOR SCALE

If we lower the 3rd, 6th, and 7th scale degrees of a major scale by a half step, we create a parallel *natural minor scale*. Two scales are *parallel* to each other when they start on the same note. In other words, they share the same "Do" or scale degree 1. Logically, the intervallic pattern between the seven notes changes as follows: whole, half, whole, whole, half, whole, whole.

3

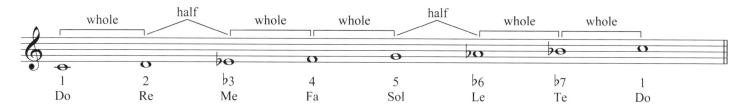

| whole | half | whole | whole | half | whole | whole |

1   2   ♭3   4   5   ♭6   ♭7   1
Do   Re   Me   Fa   Sol   Le   Te   Do

FIG. 4.7. C Natural Minor Scale

NATURAL MINOR

The reason we use the term "natural minor scale," as opposed to simply "minor scale," is because there are important variations of the minor scale, especially harmonic minor and melodic minor. We will explore them later.

If you look closely at the piano keyboard, you will notice that that intervallic pattern can be found using white notes only starting on the note A.

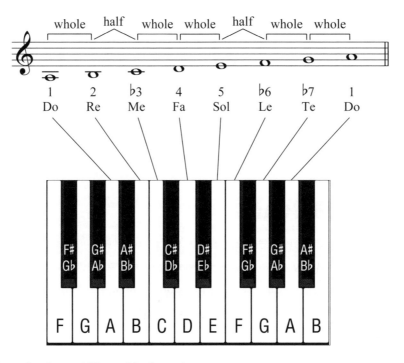

FIG. 4.8. A Minor Scale and Piano Keyboard

Since the C major scale and the A minor scale share the same seven notes, the two scales are *relative* to each other. Every major scale has a relative minor, and vice versa. There are two quick ways to find these couples:

1. A relative minor scale starts on the sixth scale degree of any major scale. Conversely, the relative major scales starts on the flat third scale degree of any minor scale.

2. The starting note (Do) of any two relative scales are situated a minor third apart, with the minor scale on the bottom and the major scale on top.

FIG. 4.9. Overlapping Scales

NATURAL MINOR SCALE DEGREES

Notice that the scale degree numbers for a natural minor scale will always be as follows: 1 2 ♭3 4 5 ♭6 ♭7 1, regardless of the need for flats on the notes themselves. The flats attached to the numbers simply reflect the difference with the parallel major scale.

DRILL CORNER

Sing up and down the natural minor scale using solfège, numbers, and letters. Switch between them halfway through. Notice that when you change to a different minor scale, only the letter names change. The numbers and solfège syllables remain the same.

PENTATONIC SCALES

A *pentatonic scale*, as the name suggests, is a scale that consists of five notes within the octave. Ubiquitous in many folk traditions, we find a wide variety of pentatonic scales around the world, each with a unique intervallic pattern. For our purposes, we will focus on the *major* and *minor pentatonic scales*, which are closely related to the major and minor scales we introduced earlier.

A *major* pentatonic scale may be constructed by omitting scale degrees 4 and 7 of the major scale. Notice that both scale degrees 4 and 7 would create a half step with their neighboring note. By omitting these two scale degrees, we effectively omit any half steps among the notes of the major pentatonic scale.

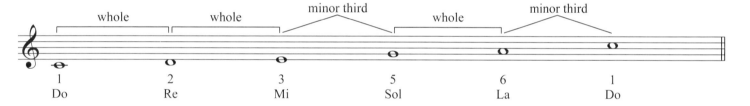

FIG. 4.10. C Major Pentatonic Scale

Listen to the opening riff in the bass of "My Girl" by the Temptations to hear the major pentatonic scale.*

A *minor* pentatonic scale may be constructed by omitting scale degrees 2 and 6 of the natural minor. Once again, by doing that, we effectively omit any half steps between the pitches.

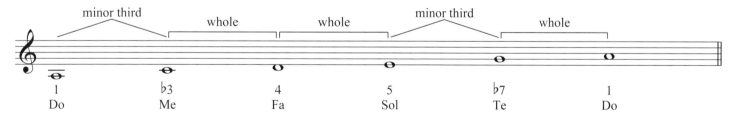

FIG. 4.11. A Minor Pentatonic Scale

Listen to "Rolling in the Deep" by Adele to hear an example of a minor pentatonic scale.**

---

* "My Girl" by the Temptations (Smokey Robinson, Ronald White), Motown, 1964.
** "Rolling in the Deep" by Adele (Adele Adkins, Paul Epworth), Adele, *21*, XL, Columbia, 2011

MAJOR AND MINOR PENTATONIC RELATIVES

A pair of two relative major and minor pentatonic scales share the same notes, just like two relative major and minor scales do.

 ASSIGNMENT 4.1

INTERVALS AS REPRESENTED IN THE MAJOR AND MINOR SCALES

Now that you have a solid foundational knowledge of scales, it is time to return to our exploration of intervals—their quantity and quality, and their relationship to the major and minor scales. The concepts described here applies to every major key, although we will use the key of C as an example.

FIG. 4.12. Intervals Up from Do in the Major Scale

Here's a different look at the same idea, using interval abbreviations (M for major and P for perfect).

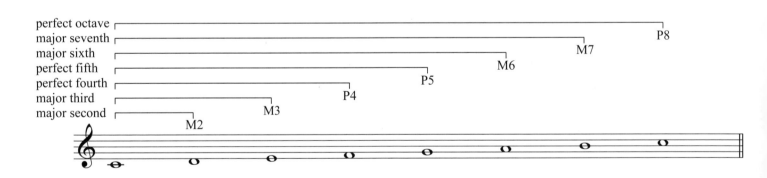

FIG. 4.13. Intervals from Do

As you can see, when ascending from the root (C in this case) of any major key, all the intervals are either major or perfect.

In a natural minor scale, all the intervals (except the second) ascending from the root are either minor or perfect.

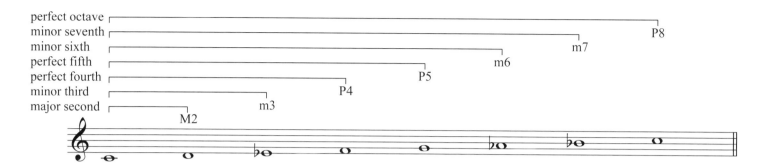

FIG. 4.14. Intervals of C Natural Minor Scale

Armed with that knowledge, you can easily determine the quality of an interval simply by knowing if the top note belongs to the major or minor key of the bottom note. In the case of the fourths and fifths, it doesn't matter if the key is major or minor—as long as the top note of the interval belongs to the key of the bottom note, the interval will be perfect.

INTERVAL INVERSION

Switching the position of the top and bottom note of an interval creates an *inversion*. Whether the bottom note is set up an octave, or the top note is set down an octave, the resulting interval will be the same.

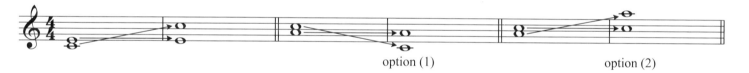

FIG. 4.15. Interval Inversion

Looking at the C major scale one more time, notice that all the intervals descending from the top C are either minor or perfect.

FIG. 4.16. Descending Intervals

This reveals the following patterns:

- The numbers for any two intervals when inverted add up to 9: a second inverts into a seventh, a third into a sixth, a fourth into a fifth, and vice versa.
- Major intervals invert into minor intervals and vice versa: a major third becomes a minor sixth; a minor second inverts into a major seventh.
- Perfect intervals remain perfect: a perfect fourth inverts into a perfect fifth.
- Augmented intervals invert into diminished intervals and vice versa.

FIG. 4.17. Inverted Intervals

Now that you understand interval inversion, mastering seconds and thirds will provide you with a quick and easy way to determine the quality of all sevenths and sixths respectively.

A handy method to determine whether a fourth or a fifth is perfect is knowing that if both notes of the interval are natural, both notes are sharp, or both notes are flat, then the fourth or fifth will be perfect. The one exception is between the notes B and F!

Memorizing the quality of the seconds, thirds, and fourths between any two white notes on the piano is a crucial step in mastering intervals. You know that enlarging the distance between two notes by half step creates the next quality up; minor becomes major, major becomes augmented, etc. Conversely, decreasing the distance by a half step creates the next quality down; perfect becomes diminished, major becomes minor, etc.

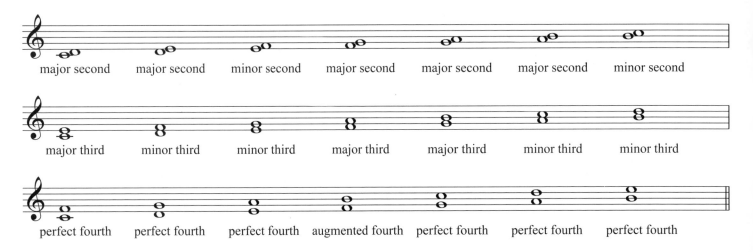

FIG. 4.18. Piano White Note Intervals in the Key of C

 **ASSIGNMENT 4.2**

CHAPTER 5

Triads

One of the most interesting, compelling, and satisfying gestures in music is playing three or more notes simultaneously and listening to the effect produced by the different combinations of pitches. These vertical structures of notes played at the same time are called *chords*. The simplest and historically most ubiquitous chords are called *triads*. A triad is a set of three notes stacked vertically (played simultaneously) in thirds.

The three notes of a triad each have a name and a role.

- The base note is called the *root*. It carries the name of the triad.
- The note above it is called the *third* (3), as it is built a third above the root. As you know from your interval studies, thirds may be major or minor. The quality of the third determines the basic quality of the triad.
- The note above the third is called the *fifth* (5), as it is built a fifth above the root. Fifths may be perfect, diminished, or augmented. The quality of the fifth fine-tunes the quality of the triad.

7

major triad   minor triad   diminished triad   augmented triad

FIG. 5.1. Major, Minor, Diminished, and Augmented Triads

Figure 5.1 shows the most common qualities of triads—major, minor, diminished, and augmented. Their interval structure is as follows:

major triad	a major third and a perfect fifth above the chord root
minor triad	a minor third and a perfect fifth above the chord root
diminished triad	a minor third and a diminished fifth above the chord root
augmented triad	a major third and an augmented fifth above the chord root

Contemporary music uses *chord symbols* to identify the different chords by root and quality. There are a few different conventions out in the world using slightly different chord symbols, and it is a good idea to be familiar with the most common ones. We will return to this topic when we explore seventh chords, where the variety is much larger. Here are the most common chord symbols for triads, each built on the note named by an uppercase letter.

C   An uppercase letter with no additional characters signifies a major triad.

Cmin   The abbreviation min signifies a minor triad.

C°   A small circle (or the abbreviation "dim") signifies a diminished triad.

C+   A plus sign (or the abbreviation "aug") signifies an augmented triad.

Note: We deliberately use both °/dim and +/aug throughout this book in order to give you practice at identifying both common abbreviations. They mean the same thing.

DRILL CORNER

1. Say the names of the three notes of a triad quickly, as if it's one word. For example, GBD. Repeat it a few times until it truly feels like a single word. Move on to another triad, until you have done all seven of them. Don't worry about sharps and flats at this time, just focus on the natural notes. Go in order, starting from C and moving up the major scale. Then go down from C moving down the major scale. Then try saying every other chord, or mix them any way you wish, but focus on speed and fluency.

2. String along all the notes in thirds until you complete the circle: C E G B D F A C. Repeat it until it feels natural and fluent, then move up and do the same starting on E: E G B D F A C E, then up again etc. until you can say this string of notes quickly and fluently starting any place you wish.

TRIAD INVERSIONS

More often than not, chords appear in root position—the root of the chord is in the bass, or lowest voice—with the other two notes stacked above it. On occasion, you may encounter a voicing of a chord where the lowest note is not the root, but rather the 3 or the 5. This is also a type of an *inversion*, and we have a special way of notating it in the chord symbol above the chord: using a slash (see figure 5.2).

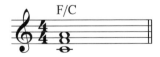

FIG. 5.2. F Major Triad in Second Inversion

If the root of the chord is played by the bass (or the left hand of the piano), while another instrument (or the right hand of the piano) is playing the full triad on top, it may look like the triad is inverted, but since we are still hearing the root of the chord in the lowest voice, that is not really an inversion but simply a chosen *voicing* (i.e., arrangement of chord notes). We will explore that concept further and cover some useful conventions in correct spelling of chords in the chapter for seventh chords later in this book. Figure 5.3 shows an example of an F chord that is still considered in root position because the bottom note is the root, even though other notes of the triad are in a different order.

FIG. 5.3. F Major Triad with the Root in the Bass

 ASSIGNMENT 5.1

CHAPTER 6

Key Signatures; Circle of Fifths

In chapters 3 and 4, we mentioned the importance of establishing a key and using a key signature as a shortcut to knowing what notes belong to each key. It is time to dig into this concept a bit deeper and start committing some of this knowledge to memory.

Essentially, a *key* is a collection of seven (out of the twelve possible) notes within an octave. The implications of this simple definition, however, are quite complex.

The seven notes that comprise a key are described as *diatonic*, meaning *belonging to the key*. They create scales—such as major or minor—that define the quality of the key. We also describe these scales (and others that follow similar relationships of whole and half steps) as *diatonic*.

Notes in the key also are used to create *chords*—vertical structures of three or more notes—that have an established hierarchy and motion tendencies called *functions*. Chords built exclusively of notes from a key are called *diatonic chords*, and are analyzed using Roman numerals (see chapter 7).

Last but not least, the seven notes of a key are used to create intervallic relationships with each other, called, you guessed it, *diatonic intervals*.

Any one of the twelve notes within an octave may serve as the foundation (or Do) of a key. *The name of the key matches the starting note + the quality (major or minor).* For example, if the starting note (Do) of a key is the note E♭ and the seven notes create a major scale, the name of the key is "E♭ major." Similarly, if it starts on the note F♯ and the seven notes create a minor scale, the key is F♯ minor. You may recall that scales may be *parallel* (starting on the same Do) or *relative* (sharing the same notes) to each other. Keys follow suit.

Key signatures indicate the collection of sharps or flats required to create a diatonic scale. The key of C major does not require any sharps or flats since the white notes on the piano create a major scale. As soon as we pick a different starting note, we will need anywhere between one and up to seven sharps or flats in order to keep the intervallic relationship of major or minor intact.

The goal is to memorize all twelve major and all twelve minor keys (plus three enharmonic spellings for each) and their key signatures. The following concepts and discussions will help you with this task.

CIRCLE OF FIFTHS

Created by Pythagoras in Ancient Greece, the circle of fifths has stood the test of time as a handy tool in understanding and memorizing the relationship between different keys.

The circle is divided into twelve points: one for each pitch within the octave. The distance from one point to the next is up a perfect fifth (going clockwise) or up a perfect fourth (going counterclockwise). Each point represents a major key, with the relative minor usually depicted inside the circle. Starting with the key of C (which has no sharps or flats), each consecutive key in clockwise direction requires an additional sharp, while each consecutive key in counterclockwise direction requires an additional flat. At the bottom of the circle we find the three keys that may be represented *enharmonically* (different name for the same note). Take your time exploring figure 6.1, and see what other patterns you notice before we continue.

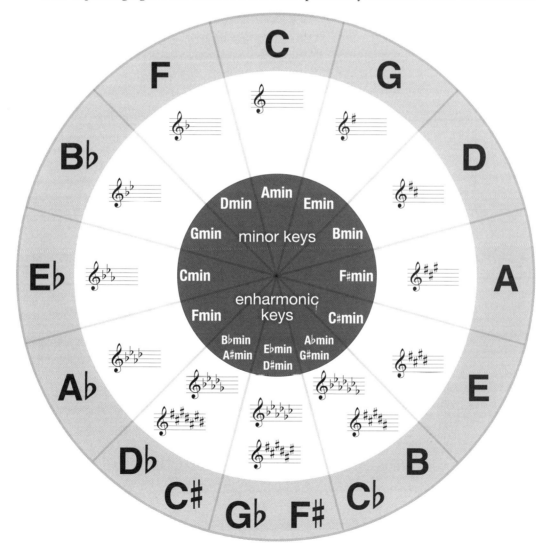

FIG. 6.1. Circle of Fifths

DRILL CORNER

Commit the following sequences by memory

- F C G D A E B (the order in which sharps appear to form a key signature)
- B E A D G C F (the order in which flats appear to form a key signature)
- G D A E B F♯ C♯ (the order of keys requiring sharps)
- F B♭ E♭ A♭ D♭ G♭ C♭ (the order of keys requiring flats)

KEY SIGNATURE TIPS

Notice that:

- The last sharp in a key signature is always the "Ti" of the major key it serves.

- The second to last flat in a key signature carries the name of the major key it serves.

Here is a different visual representation of the order of keys, sharps and flats:

1   2   3   4   5   6   7   ← the order in which each sharp appears in a key signature

F   C   G   D   A   E   B

7   6   5   4   3   2   1   ← the order in which each flat appears in a key signature

Carefully examine the lists above. What other patterns do you notice?

Finally, it is important to learn the proper format for writing down key signatures in both clefs. Pay close attention to the positioning of each sharp and flat on the staff.

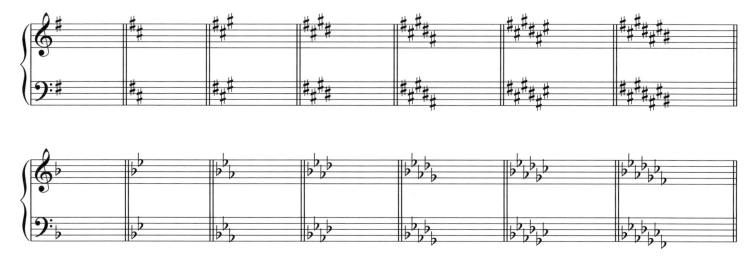

FIG. 6.2. Key Signatures. Note the order and placement of each accidental.

Every major key has a relative minor and vice versa. *Relative keys share the same key signature.* We explored this relationship when we introduced scales. As a reminder, there are two quick ways to find relative keys:

1. A relative minor key starts on the sixth scale degree of the relative major key. Conversely, the relative major key starts on the flat third scale degree of the relative minor.

2. The starting note (Do) of any two relative keys are situated a minor third apart, with the minor key a minor third below the major.

Every major key has a parallel minor and vice versa. Parallel keys start on the same note but have different key signatures. C major and C minor keys are parallel to each other. Parallel minor keys have scale degrees 3, 6, and 7 lowered by a half step compared to major. Therefore, the key signature of a parallel minor will always have three fewer sharps or three more flats (or a combination of both) compared to the parallel major key.

RELATIONSHIP BETWEEN MELODY, PITCH, AND KEY

As your ear develops, you will be able to identify how your melody note relates to the key of the piece you are playing—a valuable skill for any musician, but especially crucial for vocalists and melodic instrumentalists.

The challenge is how to recreate that awareness of key and melody relationship simply by looking at a lead sheet or score. As we've mentioned before, you must develop the ability to *see what you hear, and hear what you see.*

The simplest approach is to identify the key that you are in based on the key signature then identify the scale degree of the first melody note. Using solfège, sing the scale up from Do to your starting pitch.

For example, if the piece is in the key of E♭, and the starting melody note is G, we recognize the G as the third of the key, or Mi. Sing the major scale starting on the pitch E♭, and stop on Mi—that is the starting pitch of the melody. Over time, you'll be able to skip singing the scale and sing the interval directly.

| Mi | Mi | Sol | Re | Do |

FIG. 6.3. Melody in E♭ Major with Solfège

 ASSIGNMENT 6.1

CHAPTER 7

Diatonic Harmony in Major Keys; Roman Numerals

The term *diatonic* is an important part of your vocabulary as a musician. In the context of music theory, it simply means belonging to the key. It may be applied to single notes, scales, intervals, or chords. The opposite of diatonic is chromatic, which refers to all twelve notes of the chromatic scale, rather than the seven notes of the key signature you are in.

 Let's explore the seven diatonic triads we can build using only the seven notes of any given major key.

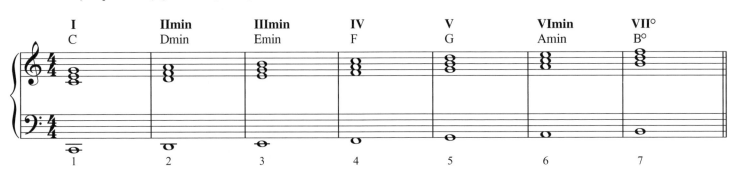

FIG. 7.1. Triads Built on Each Scale Degree of a Major Scale

As you can see in figure 7.1, three types of triads are diatonic to the major key: major, minor, and diminished. The order in which they appear is the same in every major key: the first, fourth, and fifth triads (built on the first, fourth, and fifth scale degree of the key) are always major. The second, third, and sixth triad are always minor. And, the seventh triad is always diminished. It is very important to have that order memorized and internalized.

Music is rarely completely diatonic to the same key from beginning to end. We use accidentals to expand the quality of a diatonic chord to a desired non-diatonic chord without changing the key. For example, if we want to change the second chord of the C major key from D minor to D major, we add a sharp to the note F, which changes the interval between the root and the third of the D chord from a minor third to a major third.

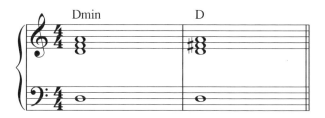

FIG. 7.2. D Minor and Major Triads: Diatonic to C Major Converted to Non-Diatonic to C Major

DRILL CORNER

Memorize the order of the triads by quality: 1 major, 2 minor, 3 minor, 4 major, 5 major, 6 minor, 7 diminished.

ROMAN NUMERALS

Notice the Roman numerals above the chord symbols in figure 7.1. Roman numerals are an invaluable tool for analyzing the harmonic makeup of a piece of music. Each Roman numeral represents the scale degree on which the chord is built, and the quality of the triad—major, minor or diminished. They are independent of the key of the piece, which makes them a great tool for transposing the piece to a different key if desired. In classical music analysis, we often see the Roman numerals written below the staff, where major chords use uppercase Roman numerals, while minor chords use lowercase Roman numerals. At Berklee College of Music, we use a slightly different convention that is better suited to the demands of contemporary music: all Roman numerals are written above the chord symbols, all in uppercase, and the quality of the chord is reflected in the Roman numeral exactly the same way it is reflected in the chord symbol—min after the Roman numeral represents a minor triad, a small circle in the upper right corner represents a diminished triad (or sometimes "dim"), and a simple Roman numeral with no additional symbols represents a major triad.

 ASSIGNMENT 7.1

TYPICAL CHORD PROGRESSIONS AND VOICE LEADING IN CONTEMPORARY MUSIC

Playing or writing chords in a particular order creates a *chord progression*.

The chord progression of a piece is an important compositional element, along with melody, rhythm, and form. Although, technically speaking, it is possible to place chords in every conceivable order, there are certain factors (such as harmonic rhythm, function, style, and genre) that contribute to writing compelling and effective chord progressions. We'll explore all of these factors later in this book, but for now, here are a few typical diatonic chord progressions for your consideration.

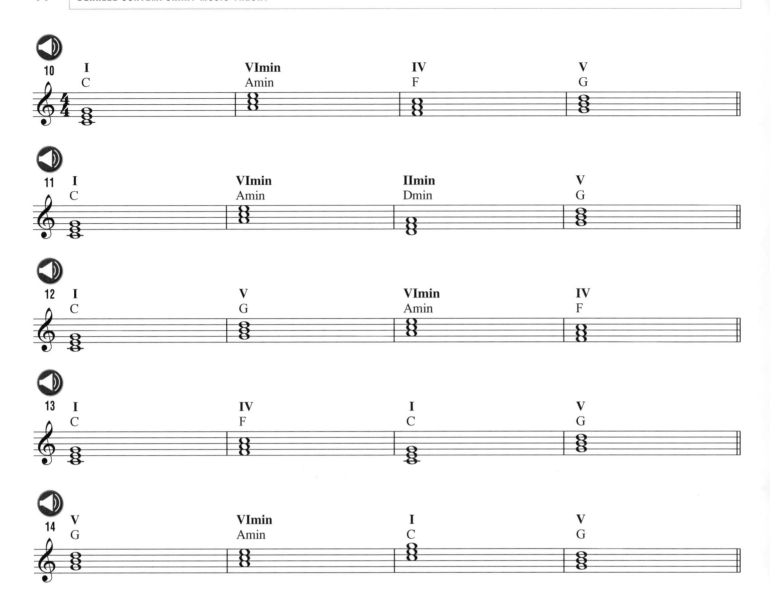

FIG. 7.3. Typical Chord Progressions

VOICE LEADING

All the chords in the chord progressions in figure 7.3 are presented in root position, which makes them easy to read. In practice, however, playing each chord in root position can create undesirable effects. If the chord progression serves as a harmonic background to an independent melody, jumping from chord to chord will pull the attention of the listener towards the accompaniment and away from the melody. If the progression is played on a keyboard instrument, playing every chord in root position will cause too much hand movement, making the progression difficult to play.

The practice of moving smoothly from one chord to the next is called *voice leading*. The word *voice* in this context has three different meanings. In one sense, it refers to each individual note of the chord as it relates to the bass: top note, middle note, or bottom note. At the same time, it refers to each horizontal melodic line created by connecting all the top notes, all the middle notes, and all the bottom notes, respectively: the top voice, middle voice, and bottom voice. Finally, the *voicing* of a chord refers to the vertical order of the notes of each chord.

Effective voice leading is achieved by inverting the notes above the bass in order to keep common notes in the same voice, move stepwise when possible, and avoid big leaps. Since the notes in the bass are the roots of each chord, the chords will remain in root position, even though their voicing has changed.

15

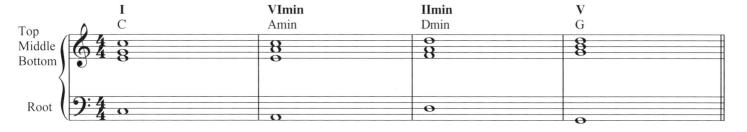

FIG. 7.4. Voice Leading Triads

ASSIGNMENT 7.2

CHAPTER 8

Diatonic Harmony in Minor Keys

Diatonic harmony in minor keys follows the same general principle as diatonic harmony in major keys—building chords in triads starting on each note of the scale. Of course, the main difference is the scale itself: minor keys use a minor scale. For our purposes, we will focus on the *natural minor scale*, for now. We will explore other variations of the minor scale (such as harmonic, melodic, and Dorian) later in this book.

16

Here are the seven diatonic triads of the A natural minor scale:

| Imin | II° | ♭III | IVmin | Vmin | ♭VI | ♭VII |
| Amin | B° | C | Dmin | Emin | F | G |

FIG. 8.1. Triads Diatonic to the Key of A minor

Similarly to a major key, the Roman numerals indicate the scale degree on which the chord is built, as well as the quality of the chord—major, minor, or diminished. The order in which the qualities appear is different from a major tonality, and requires memorization and internalization. Notice the flat signs in front of the III, VI, and VII Roman numerals. These correspond to the flats in front of scale degrees 3, 6, and 7 of the minor scale (as compared to the parallel major, or indicating the quality of the interval between Do and each scale degree respectively; see chapter 4 for further clarification).

In our earlier discussion about the major and minor scale, we talked about an important relationship between scales that share the same key signatures—relative major and minor scales. Since diatonic chords are built from the diatonic notes of the scale, it follows that relative tonalities will share not only the same seven notes, but also the same seven chords. Once again, the difference between a major key and its relative minor is the order in which these chords appear, and the Roman numerals assigned to them. One way to think of this relationship is this: the VImin chord of the major key is the Imin chord of the relative minor, while the ♭III major chord of the minor key is the I chord of the major key.

Compare the diatonic triads in the relative keys of C major and A minor and see for yourself!

FIG. 8.2. Compare Relative Major and Minor Triads

DRILL CORNER

Memorize the order of the qualities in minor: I minor, II diminished, ♭III major, IV minor, V minor, ♭VI major, ♭VII major.

 ASSIGNMENT 8.1

CHAPTER 9

Major and Minor Key Diatonic Harmony in Seventh Chords; Harmonic Function

By now, you are well versed in building and recognizing triads both in and outside a key. We are ready to add the last building block to our chords: the fourth chord tone, the 7.

We'll focus on building diatonic seventh chords first: simply add one more note a third above the 5 and your seventh chord is complete. This additional note will create either a major or a minor interval of a seventh with the root of the chord, and that relationship will determine the exact quality of our new seventh chord as follows:

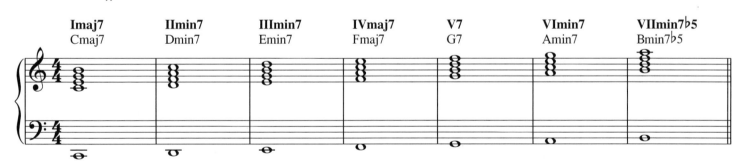

FIG. 9.1. Diatonic Seventh Chords in the Key of C Major

As you can see in figure 9.1, the major triads I and IV were transformed into major seventh chords as the interval between the root of the chord and the newly added seventh is major. The minor triads IImin, IIImin, and VImin become minor seventh chords, as the interval between the root of the chord and the newly added seventh is minor.

Where things get interesting is the V and the VII° chord. Since the triad of the V chord is major, but the added seventh creates a minor seventh from the root of the chord, the resulting chord is what we call a *dominant chord* (labeled simply as V7).

Similarly, when we add a minor seventh to the diminished triad of the VII° chord, we end up with a chord we refer to as a minor seven flat 5, labeled as VIImin7♭5.

DIFFERENT NAMES FOR CHORDS

You will find variations in naming conventions for certain chords and other music notation elements, based on region, genre, time period, and other factors.

At Berklee, what we call a dominant 7 chord is analyzed by some classical musicians as a *major-minor chord*, which is a thorough and accurate description of its structure: major triad, minor seventh.

Also, what we call a minor 7♭5 chord (min7♭5) is sometimes referred to as a "half-diminished" chord, labeled as VII°7—once again, an accurate description of the structure of this chord: diminished triad, minor seventh.

Now that we've examined all the diatonic seventh chords in a major key, let's review their structure by splitting them into two elements—the triad that results from the bottom three notes, and the interval of a seventh created between the root and the top note:

- Major triad + major seventh = major 7 chord labeled maj7
- Minor triad + minor seventh = minor 7 chord labeled min7
- Major triad + minor seventh = dominant 7 chord labeled simply 7
- Diminished triad + minor seventh = minor 7 flat 5 chord labeled min7♭5

Keen observers may wonder whether there is such a thing as a minor triad + major seventh. Hold that thought for now, we'll examine that chord later in this book.

DRILL CORNER

1. Remember the *one-word* triads: GBD, FAC, BDF etc. Continue practicing *one-word* chords adding the seventh: GBDF, FACE, BDFA, etc. Try saying each one as fast and smoothly as possible, going up and down the scale or picking the starting note at random.

2. Starting on any note, say the full scale up and down in thirds as fast and smoothly as you can: CEGBDFA, then move up to DFACEGB, etc.

3. Pick a song from the *Real Book*; any song will do, but you may want to start with something simple. Set a metronome at a slow tempo (60 bpm), and say each letter of each chord in time with the metronome, going from the root up. For example, if the first three chords are Dmin7, G7, Cmaj7, you will say the following: DFAC, GBDF, CEGB. As you get more comfortable, speed up the tempo, and add more complex chords.

INSTRUMENT ASSIGNMENT

Play the chords Cmaj7, Cmin7, C7, and Cmin7♭5, and listen carefully to the difference in quality. Transpose this exercise to different keys.

 ASSIGNMENT 9.1–9.2

FUNCTION

In addition to having a Roman numeral and a quality, each chord of the key has a specific *harmonic function*. Harmonic function refers to the role of each chord in a chord progression. Some chords feel stable and "at home." They have a *tonic function*. Other chords feel like a departure from home, or "travel time," but without too much implied tension. Those chords have a *subdominant function*. And last but certainly not least, some chords carry a lot of tension and a strong tendency to resolve to a tonic chord. They have a *dominant function*. The harmonic function of a chord is closely related to the tendencies of the notes that comprise the chord (review tone tendencies, chapter 4).

The most stable chord in a key is the Imaj7 chord, followed by the VImin7 and the IIImin7 chords. These three chords have a tonic function.

The IVmaj7 and the IImin7 chord feel like a departure from home without the pressing desire to resolve. They have a subdominant function.

The interval of a tritone created between Fa and Ti of a key defines the dominant function. The strong tendency of Fa to move down to Mi, and of Ti to move up to Do creates the effect of urgency in any chord that contains both notes at the same time. In contemporary music, the definitive dominant chord is the V7.

Imaj7	IImin7	IIImin7	IVmaj7	V7	VImin7	VIImin7♭5
Tonic	Subdominant	Tonic	Subdominant	Dominant	Tonic	(Dominant)

THE FUNCTIONAL QUALITY OF VIImin7♭5

Since the VIImin7♭5 chord also contains the tritone between Fa and Ti, it may also have a dominant function. However, it is rarely used that way outside of classical music, and for that reason, we usually leave it off the list of dominant chords.

CADENCES

The last few chords of a chord progression that form the end of a phrase, section, or the piece, are collectively called a *cadence*. Different cadences have distinct character and unlike chord progressions, a distinct name. Figure 9.2. shows the five most common cadences in contemporary music.

dominant cadence	The dominant V7 chord is preceded by the subdominant IVmaj7 chord and it resolves to the tonic Imaj7 at the end of a phrase.
jazz cadence	The dominant V7 chord is preceded by the subdominant IImin7 chord and it resolves to the tonic Imaj7 at the end of a phrase.
subdominant (or plagal) cadence	The subdominant IVmaj7 chord moves to the tonic Imaj7 chord.
half cadence	The dominant V7 chord is positioned at the end of the phrase, leaving it unresolved until the beginning of the next phrase.
deceptive cadence	The dominant V7 chord moves to any chord other than the expected Imaj7 resolution.

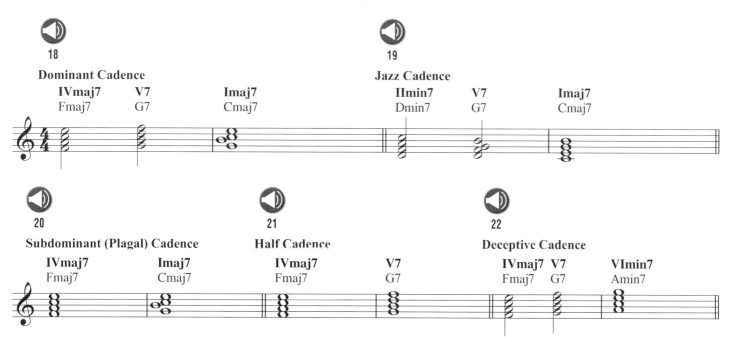

FIG. 9.2. Typical Cadences

DIATONIC SEVENTH CHORDS IN A MINOR KEY

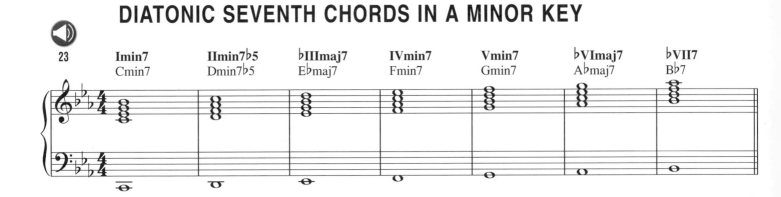

FIG. 9.3. Diatonic Seventh Chords in the Key of C Minor

Things get a bit more complex when we include the different variations of the minor scale—melodic, harmonic, and Dorian—which we will explore in detail in the second half of this book. One notable exception, which we need to address now, is the V chord in minor. Although the quality of the diatonic V chord in natural minor is a Vmin7 chord, in order for a piece to be considered in a minor key (as opposed to the modal Aeolian), we use the V7 chord, derived from the harmonic minor scale, in which the seventh scale degree has been raised by a half step to create a leading tone, and with it the familiar sound of the tritone, which creates tension that leads to resolution.

FIG. 9.4. Vmin7 vs. V7 in the Key of C Minor

VOICE LEADING SEVENTH CHORDS

Voice leading seventh chords follows the same basic rules as voice leading triads: keep common notes in the same voice, move by step when possible, and avoid leaps larger than an interval of a third. If we choose to use all four notes of the chord above an independent bass, we need to consider the proper spelling of the inverted seventh chord. The cluster (the interval of a second) that results from inverting the seventh of the chord should always have the bottom note to the left and the upper note to the right, regardless of where on the staff the two notes appear. The rest of the notes of the chord line up to the right of the stem if the stem goes down, and to the left of the stem if it goes up.

24

FIG. 9.5. Voice Leading Seventh Chords

 ASSIGNMENT 9.3

CHAPTER 10

Tensions and Avoid Notes

In addition to the four building blocks of every chord—the chord's root, 3, 5, and 7—you can add a few additional notes as color. These additional notes do not change the quality of the chord, or the Roman numeral analysis. They simply add character, and in some cases may signify a specific genre or style. We refer to these notes as *tensions*. On one hand, that name is short for "extensions," which underlines their origin. On the other hand, it literally means they add desired tension to an otherwise stable and possibly predictable chord sound.

Building tensions is easy. Simply continue stacking diatonic thirds on top of your existing chord, naming them 9, 11, and 13 (after the compound interval they create with the chord root) until you get back to the root, two octaves higher.

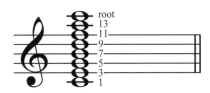

FIG. 10.1. C Major Scale Written in Thirds

The art comes in determining which of these tensions are "available," meaning that they create a desired sonic effect, and which are to be "avoided" due to the harshness of the sound (or incompatibility with the desired style) they create when combined with the chord tones around them. Notice that we don't call this a science, but rather an art, since the rules may be somewhat flexible and change over time and within different contexts. For the purposes of this book, we will present the rules for available tensions and avoid notes as historically found in the legacy of the Great American Songbook. It is your right and responsibility to explore different sounds on your own once you have mastered the basic rules presented here.

Available tensions on diatonic chords need to meet two criteria: they have to be diatonic to the key of the piece, and they must be a whole step above the chord tone below them. Since tension 9 is equivalent to scale degree 2, it needs to be a whole step above the root; tension 11, being equivalent to scale degree 4, must be a whole step above the 3; and finally, tension 13 must be a whole step above the 5.

- 9 should be a whole step above the root
- 11 should be a whole step above 3
- 13 should be a whole step above 5

The diatonic notes that do not fit the whole step above chord tone requirement are considered *avoid notes*, which means we may use them sparingly in the melody, mostly as passing tones, and avoid including them in a chord voicing when comping. We also avoid lingering on them too long, starting or ending a melodic phrase on them. For example, in C major, the 4 is an avoid note, as related to a C chord, because it is only a half-step above its closest lower chord tone, E.

FIG. 10.2. Cmaj7 with Its Available Tensions and Avoid Note

FINDING TENSIONS

A quick way to find the potential tensions is by building a diatonic triad a step above the root of the chord. Then, test each one to see if they are available or to be "avoided."

Following the two rules we outlined, here are the remaining diatonic chords in a major key with their available tensions.

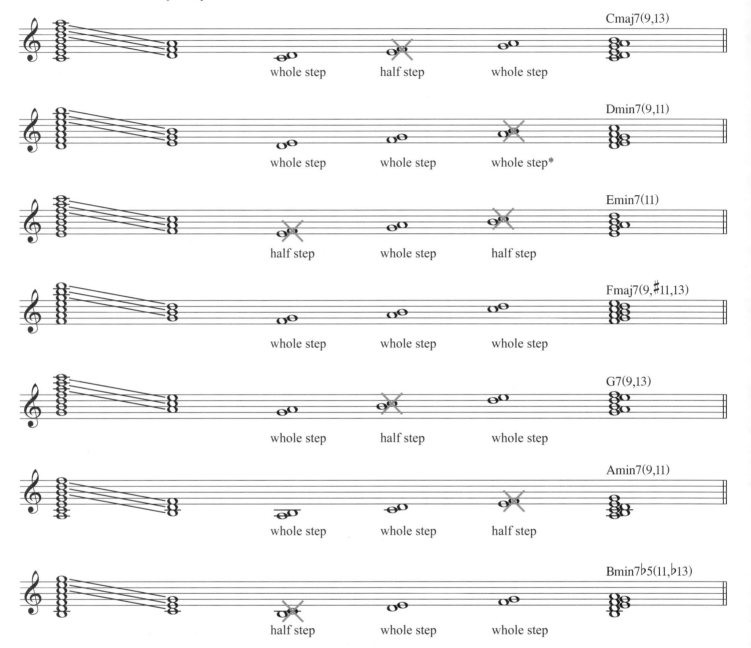

FIG. 10.3. Diatonic Chords in the Key of C Major and Their Available Tensions and Avoid Notes

Since the structure of the diatonic chords in every major key is the same, we can deduce that the available tensions will be the same as well.

- Imaj7(9,13)
- IImin7(9,11) (13)*
- IIImin7(11)
- IVmaj7(9,#11,13)
- V7(9,13)

- VImin7(9,11)
- VIImin7♭5(11,♭13)

---

* Even though tension 13 fits both requirements for being an available tension on IImin7, we often avoid using it, especially when the II chord is followed by the dominant V7 chord of the key. The reason is that tension 13, being the leading tone of the key, creates a tritone with the ♭3 of the IImin7 chord, which then demands resolution analogous to the dominant chord resolution. In effect, this tritone changes the subdominant function of the IImin7 chord to a pseudo-dominant function and thus robs the real dominant chord of its power.

Notice the ♯ in front of tension 11 in the IVmaj7 chord and the ♭ in front of tension 13 in the VIImin7♭5 chord. Adding a sharp or a flat in front of the number signifies the exact interval between the given tension and the root of the chord it belongs to. A sharp means an augmented interval, while a flat means either a minor interval or a diminished interval between the root of the chord and the tension in question.

DRILL CORNER

Memorize the list of available tensions on diatonic chords in a major key. Notice that all minor chords use tension 11, while no chord with a major third can use that tension.

INSTRUMENT ASSIGNMENT

Play the previous chords with and without tensions. Listen carefully to the change of color as you add or remove the tensions.

 ASSIGNMENT 10.1–10.2

TENSION SUBSTITUTION IN VOICE LEADING

Adding one or more tensions to the voicing of a chord will add color and character to the piece. Choosing which tensions and how many to include is often dictated by genre, personal choice, and style. Creating effective chord voicings for guitar and keyboard is addressed in chapter 12, although an exhaustive study of voicings is beyond the scope of this book.

There is one general convention however, worth exploring here as it is widely used in a variety of instrumentations. Imagine you are a vibraphone player using four mallets. Assuming you are playing with a bass player who will play the root of the chord, you have four potential notes you can use to voice the rest of the chord. If you wish to include tension 9, you will skip the root (remember, the bass player is taking care of that). If you wish to include tension 13, you will skip the 5 of the chord to free up a mallet. You should keep the 3 and 7 of the chord (also called guide tones) in your voicing as they carry the quality of the chord. The end result of this tension substitution voicing will look like this:

25

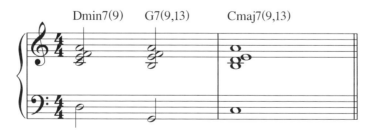

FIG. 10.4. Tension Substitution

Needless to say, you can use this type of substituting 9 for root and 13 for 5 regardless of the instrument you play or the ensemble you are writing for.

CHAPTER 11

Form Reading: Charts and Lead Sheets

The *form* of a piece of music refers to the structure of the composition. How many different sections is the piece composed of, how many phrases are within each section, do the sections repeat, and if so, how many times and in what order? In contemporary music, some examples of section types include intro, verse, pre-chorus, chorus, bridge, instrumental interlude, and coda. Different genres may have a different name for each section, but the overall ideas remain the same.

A typical song form, for example, has a 32-bar structure often referred to as AABA. Each section is eight measures long, and the A section will repeat almost identically three times in the order indicated by the sequence of the letters AABA.

Commonly, we break sections into phrases, which are usually two or four measures long. So, an 8-measure section could have two 4-measure phrases, four 2-measure phrases, or two 2-measure phrases and one 4-measure phrase.

When trying to determine the phrase structure of a piece, it is best to sing or play through the melody and feel where we naturally take a breath, or where we naturally feel a place of rest. Figuring out the phrase structure of a piece comes with experience and building a vast repertoire.

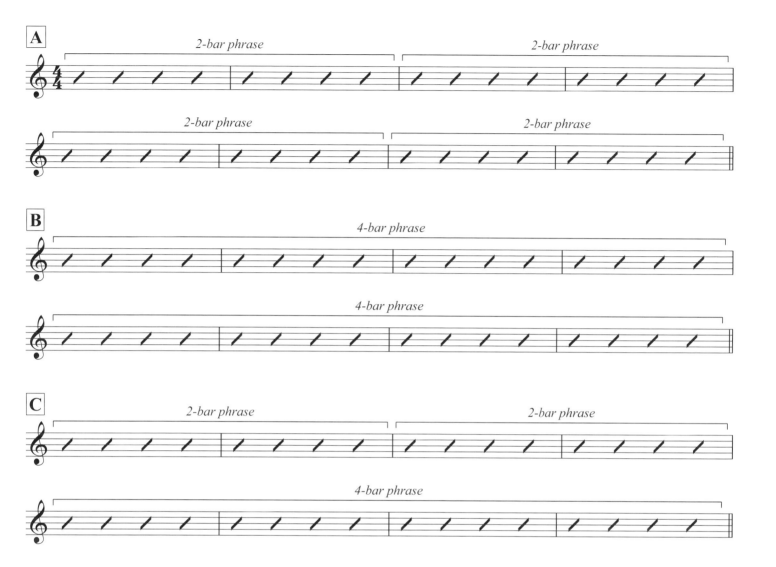

FIG. 11.1. Basic Phrase Structures: 2-Bar and 4-Bar Phrases

It is crucial to be able to follow the "road map" of a piece of music that outlines its structure, as well as to create a lead sheet of your own composition or arrangement that is clear and easy to follow. A *lead sheet* contains the melody, harmony, and form of the piece. It is usually written on a single staff that includes a clef, key signature, time signature, melody notation, chord symbols signifying the harmony, and repeat signs or other form indications.

Another important skill is lead sheet navigation. Figure 11.2. represents a lead sheet that you may see in an ensemble rehearsal. We want to look at the overall path that the use of repeats, D.S., and Coda can bring us on. The use of double bars and rehearsal letters help us outline the form.

FIG. 11.2. Basic Layout for AABA Form with Repeat Signs, D.S., and Coda

Let's break down figure 11.2.

- Intro = measures 1 to 4 (double bar indicates the end of the section).

- A section 1 = Measures 5 to 12 (first ending in measures 10 to 12 indicate they are only played first time) repeat marking brings us back to measure 5 for the second A section.

- A section 2 = The second A section is measures 5 to 9, then we skip to the second ending, measures 13 to 15, with a double bar at the end indicating the end of the second A section.

- B section = Measures 16 to 23, with a double bar at the end indicating the end of the B section, and with a D.S. al Coda at the end of measure 23 indicating that we return to the sign, located in measure 5.

- A section 3 = With the sign in measure 5, we start the third and final A section and play measures 5 to 8. At the end of measure 9, there is a Coda symbol that indicates we skip to the Coda, which is located in measure 24.

- Coda = At the coda symbol in measure 24, we play measures 24 to 26 to complete the final A section and end the piece.

The form of that lead sheet is Intro / A / A / B / A. Using repeats, D.S., and Coda allows you to move about the lead sheet in different directions as opposed to straight through the form, thus eliminating the need for multiple pages of redundant information.

Here is an example of a basic layout for an ABA form using D.C. al Fine.

V.A.

Jeff Perry

FIG. 11.3. ABA Form with D.C. al Fine

CHAPTER 12

The Role of the Rhythm Section

When we think of the rhythm section, we often think of the bass and drums first. Then we add the chordal instruments, most commonly guitar and piano or keyboards. The main role of the rhythm section is to establish the groove, or the rhythmic feel of the piece. As a result, they assume the main responsibility of keeping the tempo consistent, although that responsibility is shared by all instruments. In addition, the bass, guitar, and/or piano are also responsible for the harmonic structure of the piece.

This chapter will explore each instrument of the rhythm section in a variety of contemporary styles both from the point of view of the player, as well as the composer or arranger who may not be a part of the rhythm section.

DRUMS

The main role of the drummer is to establish the groove and keep the tempo steady throughout the piece. Drummers spend a significant amount of time working with a metronome, as well as developing independence between hands and feet. A successful drummer needs to be familiar with a variety of genres and styles, as well as be able to read notated grooves.

Writing for drums presents a unique challenge. As a composer or arranger, once we have a genre, style, and tempo in mind, we can communicate these to the drummer with a varying degree of accuracy. In some cases, it's enough to select a time signature and write, for example, "Upbeat Funk" on the chart. An experienced drummer will interpret that on their own. In other cases, we may have a very specific groove in mind, which needs to be notated precisely. We may want to include a specific tempo marking that indicates the exact bpm (beats per minute) we want.

THE DRUM SET

Understanding the different parts of a drum set and how they are played is important when trying to notate a groove we have in mind. If you are not a drummer, take a moment to familiarize yourself with a drum set and all its components.

Drum notation is different from all other instruments. Although there are quite a few variations of accepted drum notation, we will focus on the basics, and some conventions particularly common at Berklee. First, drum notation uses a percussion clef. Unlike bass or treble clef, it does not assign space to pitch, but rather the exact drum or cymbal to be played.

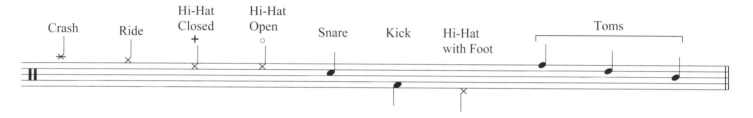

FIG. 12.1. Percussion Clef and Notation for Drums

Then, we usually identify the parts of the drum set played by the hands and the parts played by the feet. If the part is played by hands, the notes are written above the middle line of the staff, and contrary to earlier rules, the stems go up. If the part is played by the feet, the notes are written below the middle line of the staff and the stems point down.

Notice the peculiar shapes of some of the notes. Those represent the hi-hat, and a variety of different cymbals. Notice also that the snare drum and hi-hat share the same stem, since they are both played by the hands.

We are now ready to notate a few basic grooves.

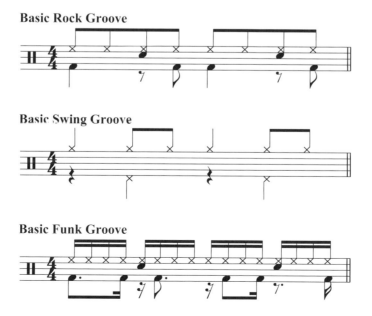

FIG. 12.2. Basic Drum Grooves: Rock, Swing, Funk

SKILL DEVELOPMENT

Drummers, play through the patterns in figure 12.2 on your instrument. All others, try clapping the top notes and tapping the bottom notes with your feet to experience the kind of dexterity required of a drummer to play these grooves.

BASS

Bass players work in close relation with the drummer, establishing the groove of the piece. In addition, the bass outlines the harmonic progression of the piece by playing roots, fifths, and sometimes other connecting notes.

An important thing to consider when writing for bass is the fact that the bass sounds an octave lower than it is written. This helps to avoid too many ledger lines below the bass clef. It is also good to be familiar with the open strings of the bass and keep in mind what the lowest available note is on a standard four-string bass.

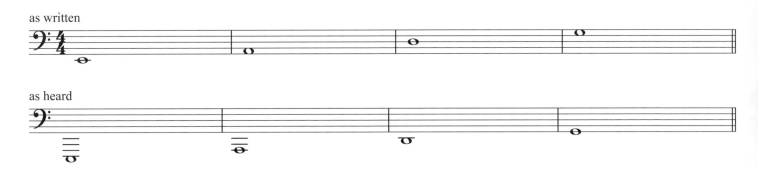

FIG. 12.3. Open Bass Notes in Concert and Transposed

When drums and bass play together, they establish a close relationship. In a rock setting, the bass may play steady eighth-note roots, which connect to the hi-hat (figure 12.4), or it may play the rhythm of the kick drum (figure 12.5). The ✗ symbol used in the drum part in measure 2 indicates that the drums repeat the exact pattern from measure 1.

Here's the bass connecting to the hi-hat:

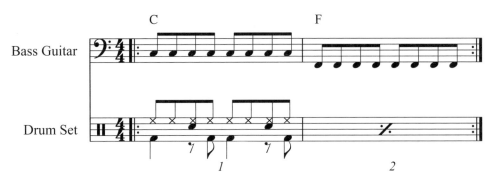

FIG. 12.4. Basic Rock Groove #1

Here's the bass connecting to the kick drum:

FIG. 12.5. Basic Rock Groove #2

SKILL DEVELOPMENT

Bass players, play through the pattern in figure 12.5, as appropriate for your level. Team up with a drummer, and play the grooves together. Pay special attention to the connection between the drum groove and your part as a bass player. Play it in different keys.

GUITAR AND KEYBOARD

As members of the rhythm section, the role of the guitar and the keyboard is to support the overall groove, and to add nuance to the harmonic structure of the song. This means playing a rhythmic pattern that agrees with the drum groove, as well as choosing an appropriate voicing of the chords that supports the genre and style of the piece.

There is an elegant way of instructing the player how to do just that while also giving them some freedom to interpret the piece on their own. It is called *rhythmic notation*. It outlines the basic rhythms of the groove using non-pitched shapes, then attaching chord symbols to the rhythms and letting the player create a voicing of their choosing. Rhythmic notation is a very effective way to communicate with all chordal instruments.

We can also use time slashes (/ / / /) in the measures following the original rhythms and *simile*, which means to play in a similar way or play a similar rhythm in this case. Each slash represents one beat.

We can use time slashes with *simile* for each rhythm section instrument. This will allow the player to stretch the time, rhythms, and groove of the original.

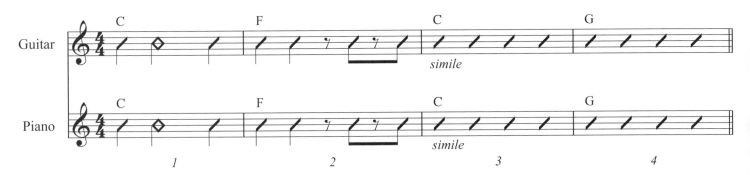

FIG. 12.6. Rhythmic and Slash Notation for Guitar/Keys

Let's put all of this together for a basic groove in a rock style.

FIG. 12.7. Basic Rock Groove for the Rhythm Section

We cannot cover all possible genres and styles here, but the following are some basic grooves most contemporary rhythm section musicians should know.

(a) Swing Groove

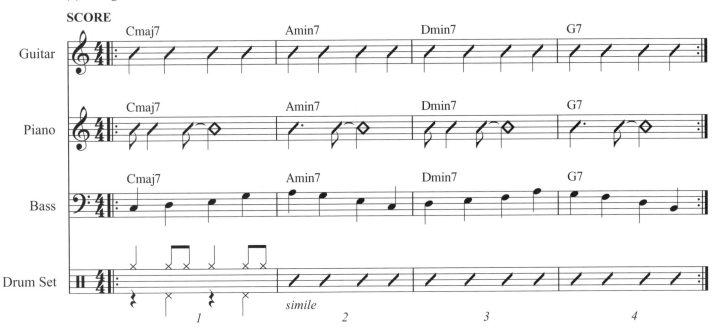

(b) Bossa/Latin Groove

FIG. 12.8. Basic Grooves: Swing, Bossa/Latin, Funk

Choosing a specific voicing to express a chord is an important skill for all chordal instrument players. It's an area of study often guided by a private instructor, and one that requires hours of practicing in order to achieve the freedom and fluidity we hear in professional musicians.

One important aspect to keep in mind is whether the chordal instrument is accompanied by a bass or not. That would determine whether to include the root of the chord in the voicing or not, as well as the register the voicing should cover.

Here is an overview of the most common voicings for piano:

Shell voicing—using only the 3 and the 7 of the chord, with or without the bass note in the left hand.

FIG. 12.9. Shell Voicings for Piano

Three-way closed voicing—using the 3, 5, and 7 of the chord if it is a seventh chord, or the root, 3, and 5 if it is a triad. The notes are close together, usually within an octave. Once again, only play the root if there is no bass player.

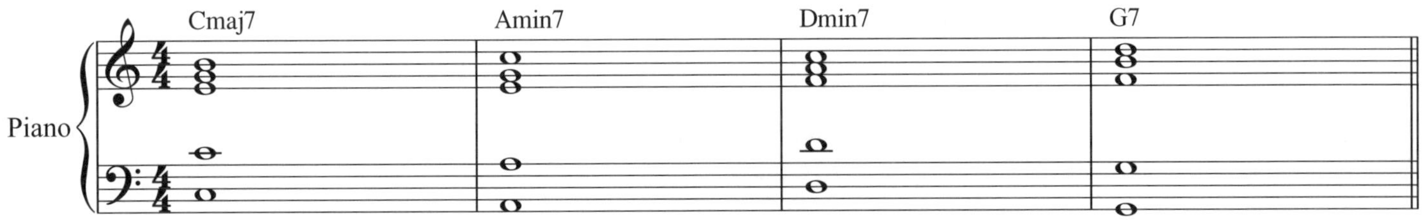

FIG. 12.10. Three-Way Closed Voicings for Piano

Four-way closed voicing—using the root, 3, 5, and 7 of the chord. The notes are close together.

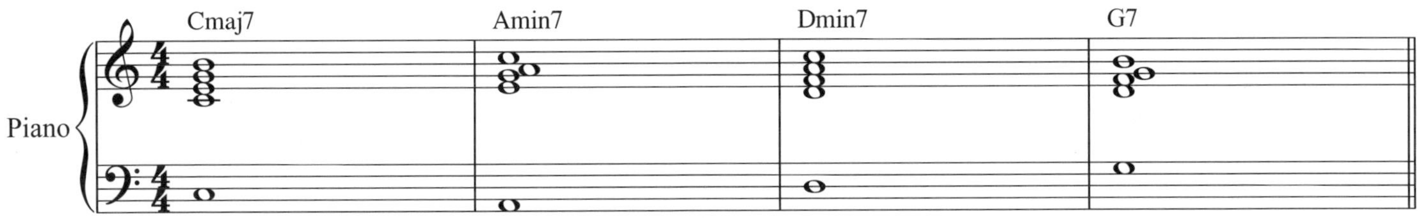

FIG. 12.11. Four-Way Closed Voicings for Piano

29

Open voicing—spreading the root, 3, 5, and 7 of the chord between the two hands, leaving space between the notes.

FIG. 12.12. Open Voicings for Piano

Writing specific voicing for the guitar is a bit more complicated. Similarly to the bass, the guitar is written an octave higher than it sounds.

It is common to write three-note voicings for guitar. The three notes don't have to be root, third, and fifth; they can be any part of the chord that you wish to use. Close position is best, meaning the three notes are within an octave. Another very important consideration when writing for the guitar is to avoid the interval of a second in the voicings. Although easy to play on piano/keyboard, seconds on the guitar are much more difficult and can involve a long stretch from one string to the next. The desired intervals for close position triadic voicings for guitar are thirds, fourths, fifths, and sixths.

FIG. 12.13. Basic Triadic Voicings for Guitar

A *drop-2 voicing* is an open voicing derived from a four-way closed voicing by lowering the second voice from the top by one octave. This helps avoid seconds.

FIG. 12.14. Basic Drop-2 Voicings for Guitar with 3 in the Lead

Both guitar and piano are versatile instruments, capable of playing a wide variety of voicings. As a guitar or piano player, it is your responsibility to explore and practice as many different voicings as possible, in all the keys. As a composer or arranger, you can learn how to write specific voicings as you develop your personal style.

It goes without saying that both guitar and piano can play melodies as well as accompaniment. Exploring how to put the two things together is a lifelong process and often what distinguishes one player from another.

CHAPTER 13

Blues Form, Progression, and Scale

Before we conclude our exploration of diatonic music and direct our attention towards various chromatic alterations, we need to address a very important and influential phenomenon in contemporary music: the blues. The single word "blues" refers to a genre, a specific form, a common chord progression, and often extends to a scale, style, and even mood.

The origin of blues as a genre is largely undocumented, but it may be traced back to the late 1800s among the African-American population in the southern United States. It is deeply rooted in the African-American work songs, field hollers, spirituals, and chants. In the beginning, the blues was simply a storytelling device sung over a single chord. Over time, it developed into the form and chord progression we now associate with it.

The most common blues form consists of twelve bars divided into three phrases of four bars each. From a storytelling perspective, the first phrase poses a question or makes a statement, the second phrase repeats the same melody and often lyrics over different chords, while the third phrase answers the question, further explains the statement, or serves as a punch line. Often, the melodic and lyrical content happen over the first two measures of each phrase, while the second half is dedicated to a pause in the melody, while the instrument *comps* (plays chords).

From a functional perspective, the first phrase is tonic (starting and ending on the tonic chord), the second phrase is subdominant (starting on a subdominant chord before moving back to tonic), and the third phrase is dominant (starting on the dominant chord and often ending with a *turnaround* back to the top of the form). This chord pattern is ubiquitous in blues.

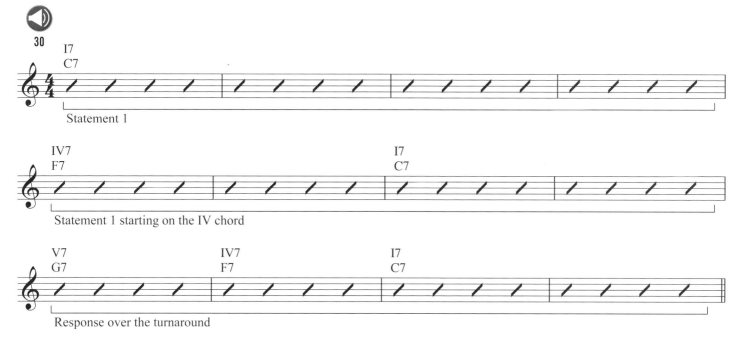

FIG. 13.1. Blues Phrasing

One of the main characteristics of blues is the use of a dominant structure (that is, including the 7) for all the chords regardless of their function. This is just one example of the unique nature of the blues.

As you can see in figure 13.1, the four measures of the first phrase use a tonic I7 chord. The second phrase is split between two measures of the IV7 subdominant chord and two measures back to the I7. The third phrase begins with a V7 dominant chord, then moves to a IV7 subdominant chord, then goes to a I7 chord for the last two measures, unless we are going to repeat the form from the beginning, in which case the last measure of the third phrase uses a dominant V7 chord to propel us back to the beginning.

 Over the years, the blues progression has undergone many variations, but the basic structure remains the same. A common variation, often referred to as a *quick change*, goes to the IV7 chord in measure 2, then back to I7 for measures 3 and 4.

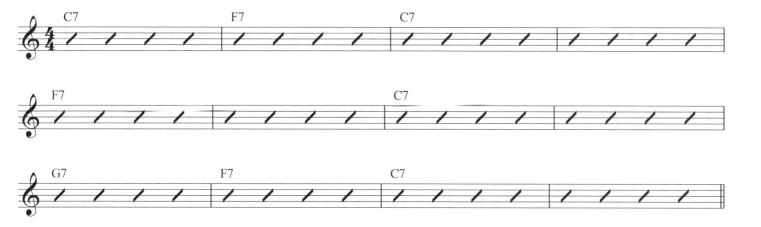

FIG. 13.2. Quick-Change Blues

Another common variation involves the *turnaround* at the end of the form—measures 9 and 10: it is very common to have a IImin7 V7 I7 instead of V7 IV7 I7. This gives the blues more of a jazz flavor. Here are a few great examples:

- "The Blues Walk" by Clifford Brown. Clifford Brown and Max Roach, *Clifford Brown and Max Roach*, EmArcy (MG-36036), 1955.
- "Blues in a Closet" by Oscar Pettiford and Harry Babasin. Bud Powell, *Blues in the Closet,* Verve (MGV8218), 1958.

32
- "Bag's Groove" by Milt Jackson. Miles Davis, *Bag's Groove,* Prestige (7109), 1957.

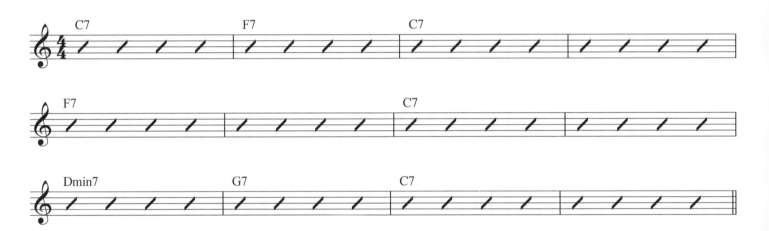

FIG. 13.3. IImin7 V7 Turnaround Blues Progression

33
Another common variation is having a minor chord sound instead of dominant chords.

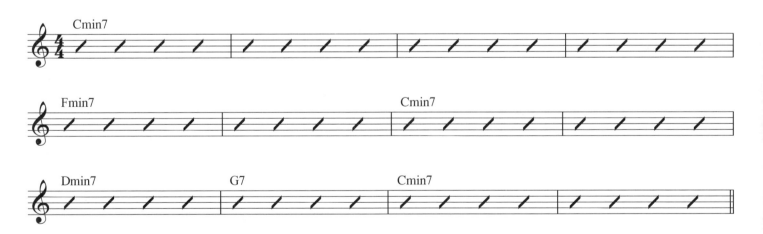

FIG. 13.4. Minor Blues

34

One more common variation that is used in all of the preceding variations is the V7 on beats 3 and 4 in measure 12, going back to the top of the form.

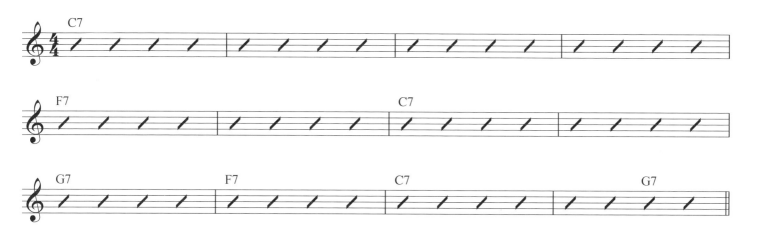

FIG. 13.5. Basic Blues Progression with V7 in Measure 12

We will discuss more reharmonization options later in the book, but these simple variations will get you very far in the blues form and style.

35

Most of the melodic content of blues originates in the minor pentatonic scale, often embellished with a ♭5 scale degree, which is sometimes referred to as a *blue note*. The resulting scale is what is widely accepted as a blues scale.

FIG. 13.6. C Blues Scale

Since blues began as an oral tradition, it is very hard to capture its essence in written notation. Sliding between notes and adding ornamentation to the melody are crucial elements of the genre. Listening to great blues artists, such as Bessie Smith (1894–1937), Howlin' Wolf (1910–1976), Robert Johnson (1911–1938), Muddy Waters (1913–1983), and B. B. King (1925–2015) is a crucial step in learning how to play the blues.

Superimposed on the dominant structured chords, we find the use of both a major and a minor third—a conflict that is often resolved by sliding or alternating between the two pitches, thus creating melodic ornamentation typical for the genre.

 ASSIGNMENT 13.1

Part II
Chromatic Alterations

The first section of this book was concerned primarily with the different elements of music theory as it focused on diatonic harmony—notes, scales, and chords belonging to one key.

In part II, we will explore the rich and exciting world of chromatic alterations. The term *chromatic* (derived from the Greek word *chromos*, meaning color) refers to notes outside of the established key that offer new colors to the music without actually modulating to a different key. Chromatic alterations are easy to spot on paper, as they require an accidental—sharp, flat, or natural. With some experience, they also become fairly easy to hear, as they deviate from the seven diatonic notes of the key.

We will start our exploration of chromatic alterations with the most common addition of non-diatonic notes, such as secondary dominants, and continue to add more and more alterations until we start to push the outer boundaries of tonality.

CHAPTER 14

Secondary Dominants and Related II Chords

Before we dig into the subject of secondary dominants, we need an important reminder: what is a dominant chord?

Going back to the structure and function of diatonic chords discussed in chapter 9, we can describe each chord with two terms: the Imaj7 chord is major and tonic, the IImin7 chord is minor and subdominant, the IIImin7 is minor and tonic, and so on.

That pattern breaks with the dominant chord; the V7 chord is dominant and well, dominant. We use the same word "dominant" to describe both the structure and the function of the chord. There is a good reason for that: most of the time, if a chord has a dominant structure, it also has a dominant function.

If you recall, a dominant structure consists of a major triad and a minor seventh from the root up. As a result, the interval of a tritone (augmented fourth or diminished fifth) is created between the 3 and the 7 of the chord. Not only does a tritone have a strong urge to resolve to a more stable interval of a sixth or a third, but the two notes comprising the tritone also happen to be the most unstable notes in the scale—Fa and Ti—both with a strong tendency to move to Mi and Do, respectively.

The V7 chord, which contains both Fa and Ti, is the primary dominant of the key. It has a strong urge to resolve down a perfect fifth (or up a perfect fourth, which for the purpose of resolution is the same—see "Interval Inversion" in chapter 4) to the chord of resolution, which we may also refer to as the "target chord."

DRILL CORNER

Answer the following questions with as many different chords as you can think of.

1. What is the dominant of _____?

   - Example: What is the dominant of Gmaj7? **Answer:** D7

2. What is _____ the dominant of?

   - Example: What is C7 the dominant of? **Answer:** F

Tip: In order to find what is the dominant of a particular chord, you simply build a dominant chord a perfect fifth above the target. If the target chord is Dmaj7, for example, a perfect fifth above that is the note A, so the dominant of Dmaj7 is A7. Conversely, when trying to determine what A7 is the dominant of, we build a perfect fifth down (or a perfect fourth up—see "Interval Inversions" in chapter 4), and we land on the target, D.

GRAPHIC ANALYSIS

The Berklee Harmony Department has developed a unique graphic analysis tool that captures the relationships between chords in a given chord progression in addition to the roman numerals attached to each chord. When a dominant chord resolves down a perfect fifth (or up a perfect fourth—the two bass motions are interchangeable for the purpose of resolution), we draw a curved arrow pointing to the target chord (or chord of resolution).

V7   Imaj7

G7   Cmaj7

 ASSIGNMENT 14.1

INSTRUMENT ASSIGNMENT

 Play the following tritone resolutions (right hand only) on the piano, and listen carefully to the effect. Then add bass in the left hand for a full dominant-to-tonic resolution. Transpose to as many keys as you feel comfortable.

36

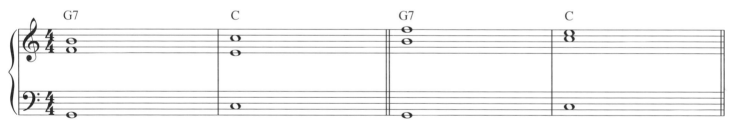

FIG. 14.1. Tritone Resolution

DRILL CORNER

If you are still struggling finding the dominant/target pairs, work on this:
- **To find the dominant when you know the *target*:** say the notes of the target chord as if they were one word, for example for a G major triad, the notes are G B D. Build a dominant chord on the last letter of the target; D7 is the dominant of G.
- **To find the target when you know the *dominant*:** say the four consecutive letters starting on the root of the dominant chord. If the dominant chord is A7, the letters are A B C D. The target chord is D.

TARGET CHORD QUALITY

A target chord may be any quality—major, minor, even dominant—while the dominant chord always has a dominant structure.

This leads us to the last set of question in this series:

1. How do I turn Cmaj7 into a dominant chord?

    Answer: Lower the 7 of Cmaj7 by a half step.

2. How do I turn Dmin7 into a dominant chord?

    Answer: Raise the 3 of Dmin7 by a half step.

3. How do I turn Amin7♭5 into a dominant chord?

    Answer: Raise both the 3 and the 5 of Amin7♭5 by a half step.

 ASSIGNMENT 14.2

SECONDARY DOMINANTS

Up until this point, we've thoroughly examined major key diatonic harmony including seventh chords with tensions, their functions, Roman numeral analysis, and typical chord progressions. Adding non-diatonic notes to a chord progression keeps things exciting and interesting. One common and effective way to do so is by creating secondary dominants.

37

Play the following chord progression (a typical "turnaround" cadence), and listen to the familiar sound:

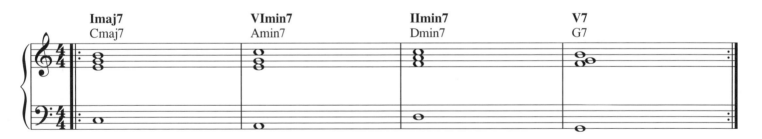

FIG. 14.2. Typical "Turnaround" Cadence

38

Now play the same progression, only this time, we'll change the quality of the Amin7 chord from minor to dominant by raising the third C by a half step to C♯.

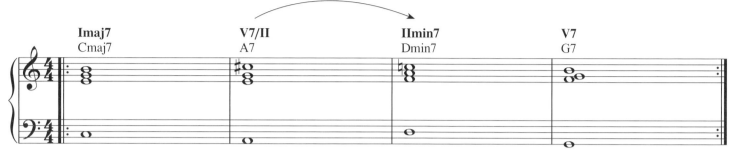

FIG. 14.3. "Turnaround" Cadence with V7/II Instead of VImin7

Changing the quality of a diatonic chord to a dominant structure by altering one or more notes creates a secondary dominant. Like all dominant chords, secondary dominants have an expectation for a resolution down a perfect fifth. The new note—C♯—is the leading tone in the key of D and has a strong tendency to move up to D. Combined with the 7 of the A7 chord (G), it creates the tritone that drives the expectation of a resolution to D. It is important, however, that we maintain the original key of the piece in this process, rather than modulate to the key of D. We achieve that by resolving the secondary dominant A7 to the diatonic Dmin7 in the key of C, positioned a perfect fifth below A7.

Alternatively, one may think of a secondary dominant as borrowed from the key in which the target chord is the tonic.

Definition: a *secondary dominant* is a dominant chord built on a diatonic root, that resolves down a perfect fifth to a diatonic target other than I.

Considering that the V7 chord of every major key is the primary dominant, we are left with six other diatonic chords that have the potential to become a secondary dominant. Upon further examination, however, you'll discover that a chord built on the 4th scale degree of the key, cannot have a resolution down a perfect fifth and land on a diatonic chord due to the inherent tritone between Fa and Ti. As a result, we are left with only five secondary dominants.

We label secondary dominant chords with a Roman numeral that clearly shows its function: V7/II, V7/III, V7/IV, V7/V, and V7/VI (pronounced "five seven of two," etc.). The arrow pointing from the dominant chord to the target chord indicates a dominant resolution down a perfect fifth.

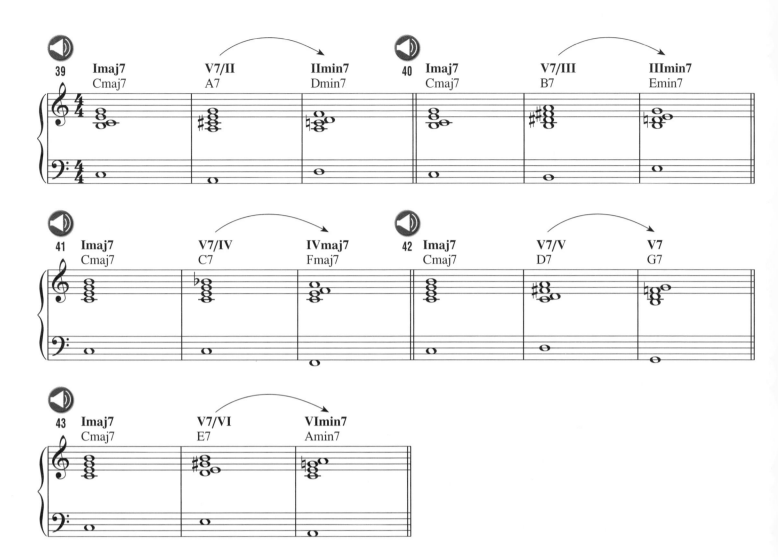

FIG. 14.4. Secondary Dominants

A secondary dominant emphasizes the role of its target chord. It creates a sense of forward motion and purpose to the chord progression. It also opens the possibility of using non-diatonic notes in the melody. In other words, one tiny chromatic alteration packs a lot of impact.

Listen to the following songs to hear examples of secondary dominants:

- **V7/IV, V7/VI, and V7/V:** "Don't Know Why" by Norah Jones (Jesse Harris). Nora Jones, *Come Away With Me,* Blue Note, 2002.
- **V7/VI, V7/V:** "Built for Love" by PJ Morton. PJ Morton, *Paul,* Morton Records/ Empire Records, 2019.
- **V7/IV:** "Lately" by Stevie Wonder. Stevie Wonder, *Hotter Than July,* Tamla Motown, 1980.

The following exercises will strengthen your ability to recognize a secondary dominant when you hear it or see it in a piece of music. They will also aid you in the process of including secondary dominants in your own music.

DRILL CORNER

Remember where each secondary dominant is built—what diatonic chord was altered in order to create the specific secondary dominant:

- V7/IV is built on Do.
- V7/V is built on Re.
- V7/VI is built on Mi.
- V7/II is built on La.
- V7/III is built on Ti.

NO SECONDARY DOMINANT ON FA/IV

As we mentioned before, there is no secondary dominant built on Fa or IV. That is because a perfect fifth down from Fa lands on Te, or ♭VII—a non-diatonic pitch. As a result, there is no such thing as V7/VII.

INSTRUMENT PRACTICE

Play all five secondary dominants and their resolutions on your instrument (or on a piano, if you don't play a harmonic instrument). Always start with the Imaj7 in order to give the secondary dominant proper key context. You may use the examples in figure 14.4. Once you are comfortable with playing them in the key of C, move to the next key.

 ASSIGNMENT 14.3

TENSIONS ON SECONDARY DOMINANTS

Since all secondary dominants are dominant chords, something they have in common is that they never use tension 11. The other two tensions—9 and 13—are available to all five secondary dominants.

The simplest way of thinking about tensions on secondary dominants is that tensions are diatonic to the *key of the piece*—not the temporary key implied by the secondary dominant, but the original key indicated by the key signature. As a result, some secondary dominants break the rule of a whole step above chord tone that ordinary diatonic chords have to adhere to. The resulting minor-second sound created by tension ♭9 with the root of the chord can be made less harsh by some strategic voicing of the chord.

Since tension ♭13 is identical with an augmented fifth, it could clash with the perfect fifth of the chord. For that reason, we usually omit the 5 of the dominant chord when using tension ♭13. On the upside, these tensions beautifully foreshadow the quality of the resolution and thus contribute to the storytelling of the chord progression.

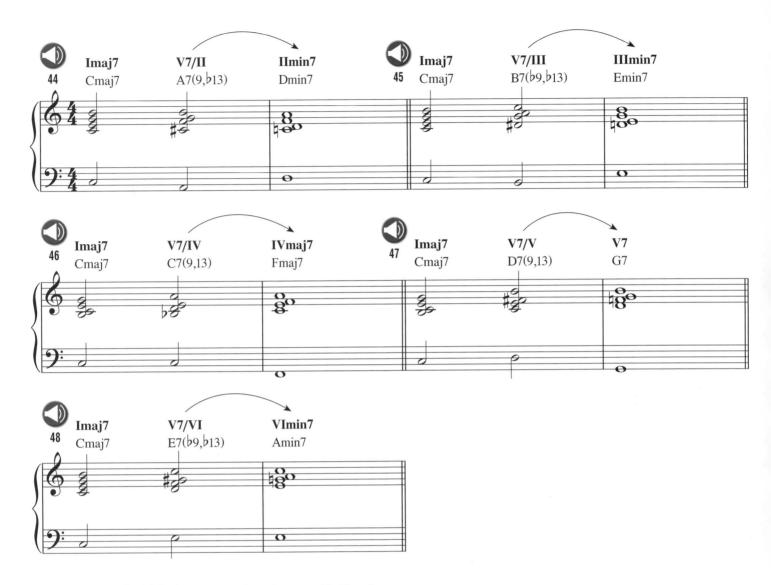

FIG. 14.5. Secondary Dominants with Tensions

If you look closely, you will notice that the secondary dominants that resolve to a major target—V7/IV and V7/V—have natural 9 and 13 as tensions, while the ones that resolve to a minor target—V7/III and V7/VI take tensions ♭9 and ♭13. V7/II also has tension ♭13, but the diatonic tension 9 is natural. In practice, however, V7/II often uses tension ♭9, even though that note is not diatonic to the key of the piece.

One final note on tensions on secondary dominants: when ♭9 is present, tension #9 is also available. Since #9 represents an interval of an augmented second, and since an augmented second sounds like a minor third, it has become common practice to use the enharmonic minor third when spelling out tension #9.

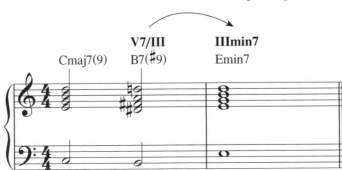

FIG. 14.6. Tension #9 (C✗) Spelled as Minor Third (D)

ASSIGNMENT 14.4

RELATED IIMIN7 CHORDS

Every dominant chord has a special relationship to the IImin7 chord of the key they both belong to. The chord progression IImin7 V7 Imaj7 is so common that it has a name: *a jazz cadence*.

The IImin7 chord is called a *related II chord*, and we use a special graphic analysis that symbolizes that bond: a bracket (see figure 14.7). Secondary dominants are indicated in the same way. They form a bond with the IImin7 chord of the key in which the dominant chord is diatonic, regardless of whether that minor chord is diatonic to the key of the piece or not.

FIG. 14.7. Related IImin7 Chords

If the related minor chord is already diatonic to the key of the piece, it has dual function. On one hand, it is the IIImin7 or the VImin7 of the key. On the other hand, it is the related IImin7 chord to the V7/III or V7/V, respectively. In the case of V7/VI, the related II chord is the diatonic VIImin7♭5. Although the quality of this chord is not exactly the same as the other related II chords, it serves the same role as the others, while also creating an expectation for a minor resolution of the secondary dominant it is related to. Remember, the diatonic II chord in minor keys is in fact a min7♭5. In practice, both the related IImin7 and IImin7♭5 chords are interchangeable.

If, however, the related II chord is not diatonic to the key, it requires no Roman numeral of its own, but simply a bracket that bonds it with the dominant chord that follows.

Needless to say, if the related IImin7 chord is not diatonic to the key of the piece, it will require accidentals when spelling it out. As a general rule, non-diatonic related II chords use tension 9 and 11 (or 11 and ♭13, if the quality of the related chord is min7♭5). The diatonic (dual function) related II chords present a choice. If the desired effect is to reinforce the original key of the piece, you may use the diatonically available tensions. However, if you wish to reinforce the temporary implied key of the secondary dominant, you should use tensions 9 and 11, regardless of whether they are diatonic to the original key.

 ASSIGNMENT 14.5

CHAPTER 15

Extended Dominants; Interpolated II Chords

Secondary dominants are usually positioned on a weak stress in the measure, resolving down a fifth to the strong downbeat of the next measure:

FIG. 15.1. Secondary Dominant Resolving Down a Fifth

One notable exception is the V7/V in the following sequence of chords:

FIG. 15.2. V7/V Resolving to V7

Since G7 is the primary dominant of the key, it is positioned on the weakest beat of the phrase. Its secondary dominant, the V7/V is then positioned on the stronger downbeat of the measure.

The phenomenon of a V7/V resolving down to a V7 chord may be extended to three or more chords following the same pattern—a dominant chord resolving down a perfect fifth to another dominant chord, to another dominant chord, to another dominant chord and so on. Each dominant chord sounds like the V7/V, and our perception of tonal center shifts with each consecutive resolution, until finally, the sequence ends with a major or minor final chord.

Rather than trying to explain each individual dominant chord as a deceptively resolving secondary dominant, we look at the bigger picture and call this type of progression an *extended dominant sequence* (and the chords within it *extended dominants*).

An important factor in creating an extended dominant sequence is the harmonic rhythm: extended dominants occur on downbeats, and the harmonic rhythm often slows down to one chord per measure, or even slower.

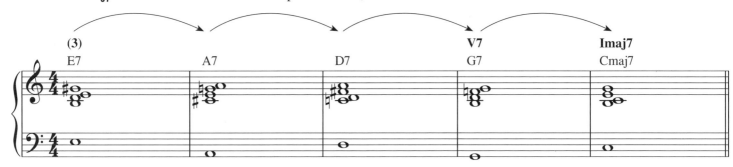

FIG. 15.3. Extended Dominants

Notice that we don't label each dominant chord individually until the last one in the sequence. Instead, we use an Arabic number in parentheses above the first chord of the sequence, which indicates the scale degree of the root of the first chord—in this case (3). Following that, we just indicate the dominant resolution down a perfect fifth without using any Roman numerals.

Since each of the dominants in the series acts like a V7/V, the tensions we use with these chords are natural 9 and 13, regardless of whether these notes are diatonic to the key of the piece.

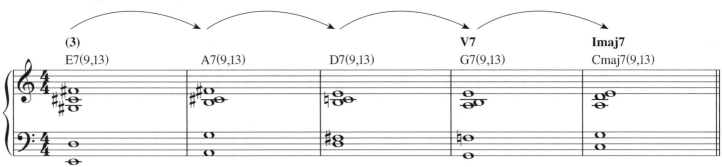

FIG. 15.4. Extended Dominants with Tensions 9 and 13

Listen to the following songs to hear examples of extended dominants.

- "I Got Rhythm" by George and Ira Gershwin. Tony Bennett and Diana Krall, *Love is Here to Stay,* Verve, 2018.
- "Jordu" by Duke Jordan, Clifford Brown and Max Roach. *Clifford Brown and Max Roach*, EmArcy (MG-36036), 1955.
- "They Won't Go When I Go" by Stevie Wonder and Yvonne Wright. Stevie Wonder, *Fulfillingness' First Finale*, Tamla Motown, 1974.

Just like all other dominant chords, extended dominants are often preceded by their own related II chords. One common pattern occurs when related II chords are added to an existing extended dominant sequence. Notice that the resolution from dominant to dominant still remains, but it is delayed by the related II chord, which has been inserted—*or interpolated*—between the two dominant chords.

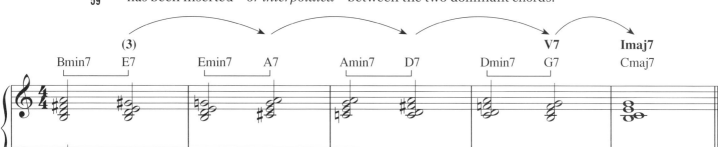

FIG. 15.5. Extended Dominants with Interpolated II Chords

CHAPTER 16

Compound Minor Key Harmony Using Seventh Chords

 60 Earlier in this book, we discussed the diatonic chords in natural minor (see chapter 8 for triads and chapter 9 for seventh chords). Here is a quick review of the diatonic seventh chords:

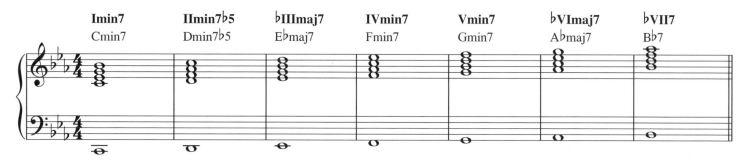

FIG. 16.1. Diatonic Seventh Chords in Natural Minor

One important characteristic of the minor scale is that it has multiple variants in which scale degrees 6 and 7 may be altered. Here are the most common variations of the minor scale.

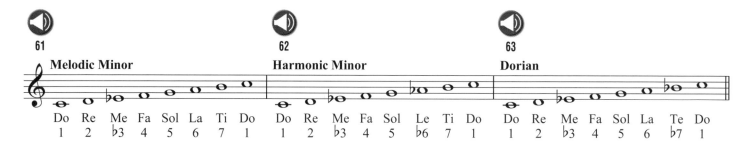

FIG. 16.2. Minor Scale Variations

In practice, minor-key pieces rarely stay within the confines of a single scale. In fact, the harmonic minor scale is imperative in order to create a V7 in place of the Vmin7. We often find other chords derived from the other scales within the same piece. Combining all the potential notes into one rich minor scale is called *compound minor.*

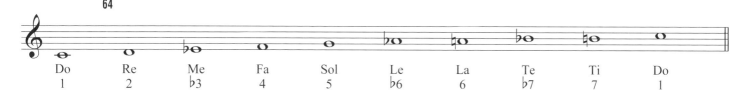

FIG. 16.3. Compound Minor

Using all the notes of the compound scale, we can now create a few variations of the familiar chords diatonic to the natural minor.

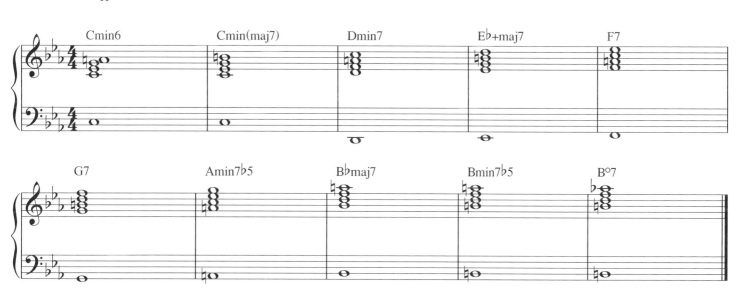

FIG. 16.4. Most Commonly Used Chords from Compound Minor

Here is a comprehensive list of the most commonly used chords in a minor key and the source scale that produced each chord.

Chord	Natural Minor	Harmonic Minor	Melodic Minor	Dorian
Imin7	•			•
Imin6			•	•
Imin(maj7)		•	•	
IImin7♭5	•			
IImin7			•	•
♭IIImaj7	•			
♭III+maj7			•	
IVmin7	•			
IV7			•	•
Vmin7	•			•
V7		•	•	
♭VImaj7	•			
VImin7♭5			•	•
♭VII7	•			
♭VIImaj7				•
VIImin7♭5			•	
VII°7		•		

Notice that in some cases, there are two potential source scales that produce the same chord. If we are only concerned with the four chord tones of the chord, the source may not really matter. However, when we look at the tensions each source scale has to offer, the significance of the source scale becomes apparent. For example, the Imin7 chord may be derived from both the natural minor and the Dorian scales. In the key of C minor, that chord is Cmin7. If using the natural minor as a source, we cannot use tension 13 on this chord since the A♭ is a half step above the fifth of the chord, G. If we use the Dorian scale, however, the A natural becomes an available tension 13, since it is a whole step above the 5 (see chapter 10 for the tension availability rule).

We will come back to this idea later in this book when we explore chord scales in detail.

 ASSIGNMENT 16.1

HARMONIC FUNCTION IN MINOR KEYS

Similarly to major keys, the three harmonic functions in minor are tonic, subdominant, and dominant. The Imin7 and the ♭IIImaj7 chords are considered stable and have a tonic function. The V chord is considered dominant only when the structure of the chord is actually dominant (V7, coming from harmonic minor), but not when it is a minor chord (Vmin7, coming from natural minor).

By far, the largest category of chords in minor is subdominant. One school of thought is that if a chord contains the ♭6 scale degree of the key, it has a subdominant function. The list includes the IImin7♭5, IVmin7, ♭VImaj7, even ♭VII7. In addition, the IV7 chord derived from melodic minor or Dorian also has a subdominant function, even though it contains a natural 6 scale degree and has a dominant structure.

Understanding and internalizing harmonic function is a lifelong endeavor, and we will continue to elaborate on it for the duration of this book.

 ASSIGNMENT 16.2

CHAPTER 17

Modal Interchange

Another common practice in music that invites notes from outside the key is borrowing chords from a parallel scale. This phenomenon is called *modal interchange*, and as the name suggests, it may include borrowing chords from any parallel mode. The most common occurrence of modal interchange is when a major key borrows from the parallel minor.

PARALLEL KEYS

Remember, parallel keys share the same Do but have different key signatures.

Play the following progression, and listen closely to the change of color when you get to the Fmin7 chord.

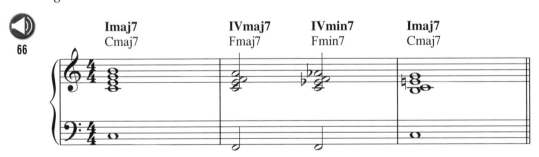

FIG. 17.1. IVmin7 Used in a Major Key

Modal interchange chords add color and nuance to the chord progression that would be unavailable if we are limited to the seven diatonic chords. They serve as an important storytelling tool, while also providing interesting and compelling bass patterns and generally enrich the harmonic language of the piece. Major keys tend to borrow from minor keys far more frequently than the other way around. The function of the chords most often borrowed is subdominant. Occasionally the tonic Imin7 and ♭IIImaj7 chords may be borrowed as well.

One of the most ubiquitous modal interchange chords is the IVmin (or IVmin7) chord. It often appears either instead of, or right after the IVmaj7 chord. It carries a minor subdominant function and a subjectively darker quality, often underlining a lyric that represents a darker emotion.

Listen to the following examples:

- **I V I IVmin I V I.** "Music Box" by Regina Spektor. Regina Spektor, *Begin to Hope (Deluxe Edition),* Sire 9362-44112-2, 2006.
- **IVmaj6 IVmin6.** "Lately" by Stevie Wonder. Stevie Wonder, *Hotter Than July,* Tamla Motown, 1980.
- **I III IV IVmin.** "Creep" by Radiohead. Radiohead, *Pablo Honey,* Parlophone-Capitol, 1993.
- **I VImin IVmin I.** "Ain't It the Life" by Foo Fighters. Foo Fighters, *There Is Nothing Left to Lose,* Roswell-RCA, 1999.

Another common modal interchange chord, also carrying a minor subdominant function is the ♭VImaj7. It may appear by itself, often followed by the V7 chord, thus creating a familiar cadence of subdominant/dominant motion. It may also be followed by another modal interchange chord ♭VII7, creating a typical minor cadence before returning to the Imaj chord.

- **Imaj7 ♭VImaj7 V7 Imaj7.** "Sir Duke" by Stevie Wonder. Stevie Wonder, *Songs in the Key of Life,* Tamla Motown, 1976.
- **♭VI V7 and ♭VI ♭VII7 I.** "All I Wanna Do" by Sheryl Crow. Crow, Cooper, Bottrell, Baerwald, Gilbert, Sheryl Crow, *Tuesday Night Music Club,* A&M, 1993.

A fairly common modal interchange chord derived from the parallel Phrygian mode is the ♭IImaj7 chord, often followed by the ♭IIImaj7 chord as in the well-known flamenco gesture of Imaj7 ♭IImaj7 ♭IIImaj7 ♭IImaj7 Imaj7. It may also appear as a passing chord between IImin7 and Imaj7.

- **IImin7 ♭IImaj7 Imaj7.** "New York State of Mind" by Billy Joel. Billy Joel, *Turnstiles,* Family Productions/Columbia, 1976.

The IImin7♭5 chord is sometimes employed in a major key, usually followed by a V7(♭9,♭13) chord for a darker and more introspective minor cadence, which when resolved to a Imaj7 chord, creates the sense of deceptive resolution, even though the bass motion is the predictable II V I.

"Here's that Rainy Day"* has a plethora of modal interchange chords, including the IImin7♭5 V7(♭9,♭13) cadence mentioned.

The Imin7 is also possible as a modal interchange chord, but if used too often it may obscure the overall mode of the piece. Use sparingly.

---

* "Here's That Rainy Day" by Jimmy Van Heusen and Johnny Burke, Bill Evans, *Alone,* Verve, 1968.

The Vmin7 chord is rarely used as a modal interchange chord, as the V7 chord carries the dominant function of the key and is therefore more powerful as a cadential chord. We often encounter what appears to be a Vmin7 chord followed by the V/IV, which is a II V cadence with the Vmin7 chord being the related II to the V7/IV and therefore does not warrant a Roman numeral analysis.

67

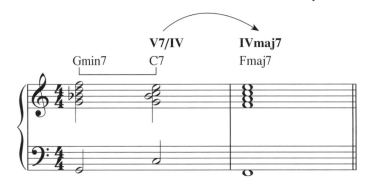

FIG. 17.2. V7/IV and Its Related IImin7 Chord

In summary, here is a list of the most common modal interchange chords:

- IVmin7
- ♭VImaj7
- ♭VII7
- ♭VIImaj7
- IImin7♭5
- ♭IImaj7
- ♭IIImaj7
- Imin7
- Vmin7

 ASSIGNMENT 17.1–17.2

CHAPTER 18

Melodic Development: Approach Notes

The art of composing, arranging, and improvising is dedicated to finding compelling ways to combine melody and harmony. An important aspect of music theory is exploring that relationship.

Melodic development is a technique used to embellish an existing melody. The melodic variations achieved through melodic development may create desired surprise, enrich the implied harmony by adding tensions to the chords, or emphasize a specific style. A well-established tool of melodic development is the use of approach notes.

Approach notes are relatively short in duration, fall on a relatively weak beat, and move by step to the target note.

As long as they meet these three criteria, approach notes may be any note of the scale—avoid note, available tension, or even a chord tone. They embellish the melody by connecting the main notes in a number of different ways, as explored in figure 18.1. If we omit the approach notes, the essence of the melody will remain intact.

The following is a list of the most commonly used approach notes:

1. Passing tones
   - Diatonic passing tones
   - Chromatic passing tones
   - Double chromatic approach

2. Neighbor tones
   - Upper neighboring tones
   - Lower neighboring tones

3. Indirect approach or enclosure

4. Unprepared approach
   - Preceded by a rest
   - Preceded by a leap
   - Preceded by itself

Listen to the examples of approach notes in figure 18.1.

FIG. 18.1. Approach Notes

The key is to experiment with these techniques, get comfortable with them, and then employ them within a melody. Play through these different types of approach tones on your instrument, sing them, get them in your ear, then write a simple melody and try using a few of the techniques you just learned.

 ASSIGNMENT 18.1

CHAPTER 19

Substitute Dominants and Related II Chords; Extended subV7s

In chapter 14, we discussed the nature of the dominant chord, the importance of the unstable tritone created between chord tones 3 and 7 (the unstable Fa and Ti of the key), and its strong urge to resolve to a more stable interval of a third or sixth.

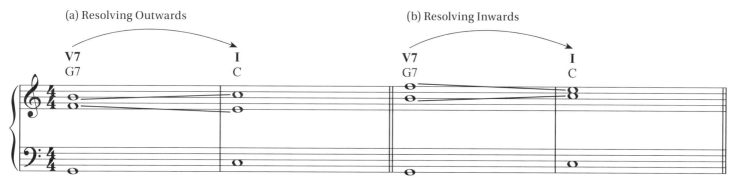

FIG. 19.1. A Dominant Chord Resolving First Outward to a Sixth and Then Inwards to a Third

This tendency of the tritone to resolve inward and outward is unaffected by its inversion, which means that every tritone has two potential resolutions:

FIG. 19.2. The Perfect Symmetry of the Tritone Allows Two Potential Resolutions

Historically, composers and arrangers have explored this ability of the tritone to resolve two different ways by substituting the two possible roots implied by the tritone. In figure 19.3, you can see that G7 and D♭7 share the same tritone and thus may substitute for each other. The graphic analysis we use to indicate a dominant chord resolving down a half step is a dotted arrow.

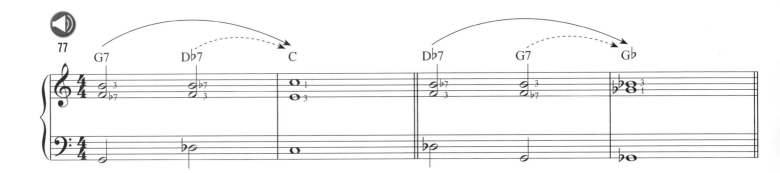

FIG. 19.3. Tritone Substitution

Notice that the tritone of G7 and Db7 is exactly the same—F and B (or Cb enharmonically spelled)—although the roles of the 3 and b7 are reversed. This means that the two chords share similar function and resolution, allowing them to substitute for each other. The roots of the two chords are also a tritone away from each other, which is a convenient way to find substitute couples. This practice is called *tritone substitution*. The non-diatonic chord replacing the original dominant is called a *substitute dominant*, and it is labeled as a subV7.

The origins of this harmonic gesture may be traced back to the Romantic music by composers such as Debussy and Ravel using the "French sixth," which is similar in structure and function to a substitute dominant.

When a bass player plays a chromatic approach note over a dominant chord by a half step from above, while a comping instrument sustains the tritone of the dominant chord, the effect is exactly the same as replacing the original chord with a substitute dominant chord. The practice of substituting one dominant chord for another has become widely spread among songwriters, composers, arrangers, and improvisors of contemporary music.

Every major key has six potential substitute dominants: the primary dominant, and five secondary dominants.

In some ways, substitute dominants follow similar rules and enjoy similar privileges as regular dominant chords:

- They usually appear on a weak beat.
- They may be preceded by a related II chord (although there are some subtleties here we need to address!).
- They can be described by a similar graphic analysis. In this case, a dotted arrow is used to show the chromatic root motion towards the chord of resolution.
- They can create an *extended substitute dominant pattern* by using chromatic root motion.

In other ways, substitute dominants are different than secondary dominants:

- Their tensions are not necessarily diatonic to the key.
- Their tensions don't vary depending on the quality of the target chord.
- Their roots are non-diatonic to the original key, with the exception of the subV7/III, which is built on Fa.

78
Substitute dominants may take the place of the original dominant or they may be interpolated between the original dominant chord and the chord of resolution:

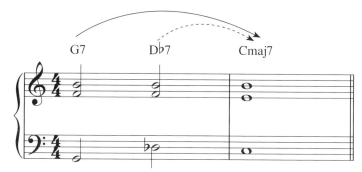

FIG. 19.4. V7 Followed by subV7 Before Resolving to Imaj7

79
Substitute dominants may be preceded by the related II chord *left behind* by the original dominant:

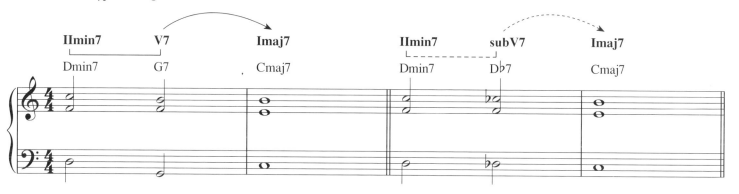

FIG. 19.5. subV7 Preceded by the Related II Chord of the Original Dominant

The new relationship between the original related II chord and the substitute dominant is labeled with a dotted bracket. Similar to the dotted arrow, a dotted bracket indicates a chromatic motion in the bass between the related minor II chord and the dominant.

Sometimes, the substitute dominant may *bring* its own related II chord:

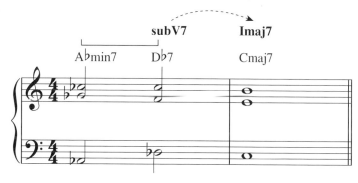

FIG. 19.6. subV7 with Its Own Related II Chord

In figure 19.6, since the A♭min7 chord is not diatonic to the key of C major, it is left without a Roman numeral. The only analysis necessary is the bracket that bonds it with the subV7.

Let's take a closer look at each secondary substitute dominant and its related II chord.

subV7/II

The subV7/II is built a half step above the IImin7 chord and a tritone away from the V7/II chord. In addition to the non-diatonic root, the subV7/II brings two more non-diatonic pitches within its structure, thus offering a lot of color to the progression.

The related II chord left by the original V7/II chord is the diatonic IIImin7 of the key. It is a dual-functioning chord, and its analysis requires both a Roman numeral and a dotted bracket showing the chromatic root motion towards the substitute dominant chord:

81

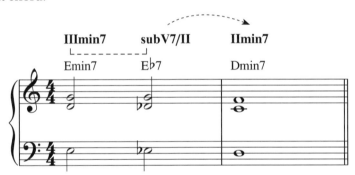

FIG. 19.7. subV7/II Preceded by the Related II Chord Left There by the V7/II in the Key of C Major

subV7/III

The subV7/III is the only secondary subV7 chord built on a diatonic root—the Fa of the key. In the event that this chord is positioned on a strong beat and not preceded by a related II chord, it is likely that it would be analyzed as a IV7 chord—either as a modal interchange from melodic minor or Dorian, or as a blues chord. In order for the secondary dominant function to be expressed fully, the subV7/III is often interpolated between the original V7/III and the resolution, or at the very least preceded by its related II chord. The related II chord has a min7♭5 quality, foreshadowing the minor resolution.

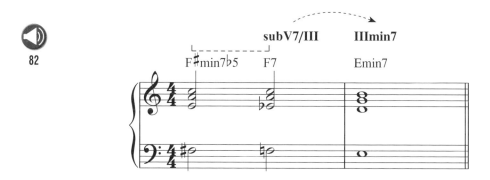

FIG. 19.8. subV7/III with Its Chromatically Related II Chord in the Key of C Major

subV7/IV

The subV7/IV chord is built on the ♭5 scale degree of the key—a half step above the resolution and a tritone away from the original V7/IV chord:

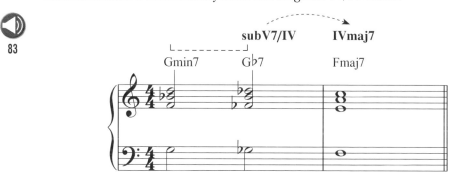

FIG. 19.9. subV7/IV Preceded By Its Chromatically Related II Chord in the Key of C Major

Similar to the subV7/II, the G♭7 brings in three non-diatonic notes to the progression. Unlike the subV7/II, the related II chord is not diatonic to the key and therefore does not require a Roman numeral.

subV7/V

Built on the ♭6 scale degree, a half step above the resolution and a tritone away from the original V7/V, this substitute dominant brings three non-diatonic pitches, and has a dual-functioning chromatically related II chord:

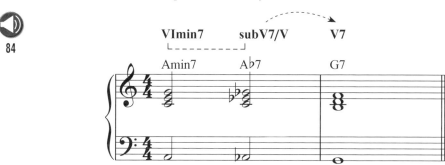

FIG. 19.10. subV7/V with Its Chromatically Related II Chord in the Key of C Major

subV7/VI

85

Although it is built on the non-diatonic scale degree ♭7 of the key, the subV7/VI shares similar issues with the subV7/III—namely, it may be confused with the modal interchange ♭VII7.

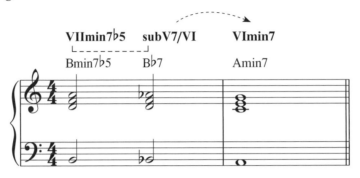

FIG. 19.11. subV7/VI with Its Chromatically Related II Chord in the Key of C Major

Just like there was no V7/VII, there is no subV7/VII as well.

Substitute dominants in minor keys follow the same logic as in major keys, but by now, it should come as no surprise that things here are a bit more complicated.

subV7/II IN A MINOR KEY

Built on the ♭3 scale degree of the minor key, this chord may just as easily be considered V7/♭VI. The analysis depends on the resolution.

86

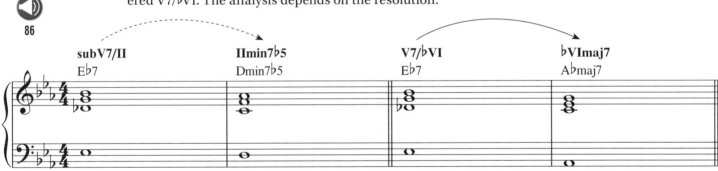

FIG. 19.12. subV7/II vs. V7/♭VI in a Minor Key

Listen to the following songs to hear examples of substitute dominants:

- **subV/IV.** "Built for Love" by PJ Morton. (PJ Morton) PJ Morton, *Paul,* Morton Records/Empire Records, 2019.
- **subV7/IV.** "Still on My Brain" by J. Timberlake, H. Mason, Jr., D. Thomas. Justin Timberlake, *Justified,* Jive Records, (2002).
- **subV7/♭VII and subV7/♭VI (deceptive).** "One Note Samba" by Antônio Carlos Jobim, Newton Mendonça. Kate Ceberano, *Kate Ceberano and Her Septet,* Festival Records, 1986.

Before we leave the topic of subV7 chords, there is one more common harmonic gesture to explore: the *extended subV7* pattern. Similar to extended dominant chords resolving down a perfect fifth to another dominant chord, the subV7 extended pattern is built by a number of dominant chords resolving down a half step to another dominant chord, thus creating the familiar sound of extended dominants, where each dominant resolves to the next.

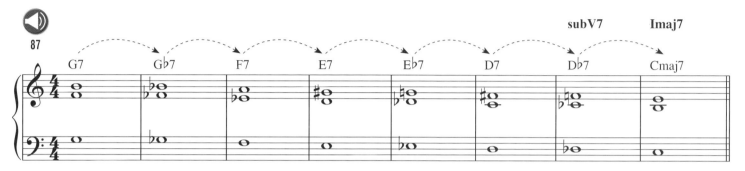

FIG. 19.13. Extended Substitute Dominants

 ASSIGNMENT 19.1–19.2

CHAPTER 20

Standard Deceptive Resolution of the Primary Dominant

A *deceptive resolution* occurs when the primary dominant of the key resolves to a chord other than the tonic situated a perfect fifth below it. This phenomenon adds an element of surprise and variety to the composition or arrangement, while still maintaining the sense of tension and release we explored in earlier chapters. The fine balance between predictability and surprise is achieved by choosing a chord of resolution that contains the stable degrees of the key—Do, Sol, or Mi—and voice leading the tritone of the dominant chord—Fa and Ti—predictably to one of the aforementioned stable degrees.

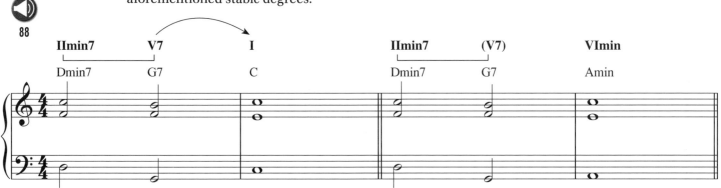

FIG. 20.1. Deceptive Resolution to the VImin Chord

As you can see in figure 20.1, the tritone Fa-Ti of the G7 chord resolves to Mi-Do of the key, whether the chord of resolution is the I chord C or the VImin chord Amin. In the case of the C chord, these are the 3 and root of the chord, while in the case of the Amin chord, they are the 3 and 5. The root motion here is no longer down a fifth, which is why the arrow is replaced by parenthesis, indicating the deceptive resolution. As a result, our ear will still perceive the sense of resolution created by the motion of Fa to Mi and Ti to Do respectively, while we also get the element of surprise by the unexpected root motion and the minor quality of the chord of resolution. Since the function of the Amin chord is still tonic, this particular deceptive resolution is common and therefore fairly predictable.

There are a few good reasons to explore deceptive resolution:

- extending the ending of a tune while adding unexpected color to the final cadence
- reharmonizing a phrase upon repeat to avoid predictability (make sure of course that the melody agrees with the new chords)
- facilitating a modulation or temporary tonicization to a distant key
- creating a compelling and surprising bass line

Let's take a look at a few standard deceptive resolution chords that can help achieve the gestures described, while still fulfilling the sense of resolution in which at least one of the two notes of the dominant tritone will resolve to Do, Mi, or Sol of the key.

FIG. 20.2. Standard Deceptive Resolutions

Here is a list of the most common standard deceptive resolution chords:

- VImin7
- IIImin7
- IVmin7
- ♭VImaj7
- ♭IIImaj7
- ♭IImaj7
- #IVmin7♭5
- ♭VIImaj7

Listen to the following songs for examples of deceptive resolution:

- **V to VImin.** "Nothing Compares to You" Sinéad O'Connor. (Prince), Sinéad O'Connor, *I Do Not Want What I Haven't Got,* Chrysalis, 1990.
- **V7 to ♭VImaj.** "Every Little Thing She Does Is Magic" by the Police, Sting. The Police, *Ghost in the Machine,* A&M, 1981.
- **V7/V to I.** "Here Comes the Sun" by George Harrison. The Beatles, *Abbey Road,* Apple, 1969.

 ASSIGNMENT 20.1

CHAPTER 21

Chord Scale Theory; Modes

Chord scale theory is a contemporary method of representing the vertical structure of a chord into a linear set of pitches that contains all the potential possibilities for improvisation, creative chord voicings, and new arranging ideas. It was necessitated by the nature of jazz, where the same chord progression may be expressed in a variety of ways based on historical and individual style, personal choice, and interaction among the musicians during a performance.

In essence, chord scale theory is an interpretation of the chordal material we've already covered in this book, only looking at it from a different angle.

A *chord scale* is a scale attached to a chord. It includes the chord tones, the available tensions, and the implied avoid notes. In some situations, a chord may only have one potential chord scale available, while in other cases, the skilled musician may be able to choose from a list of a few potential chord scales. We will explore these choices in detail.

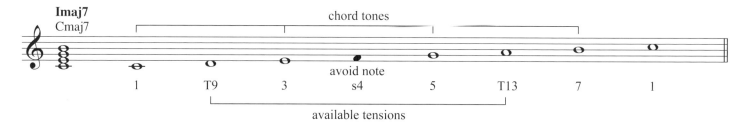

FIG. 21.1. A Breakdown of the Chord Scale Attached to Cmaj7

Here are some conventions for analyzing and labeling the different types of notes that are included in a chord scale:

- **Chord tones** are self-explanatory and non-negotiable: in order to match a chord scale with a chord, it must contain the chord tones of the chord. They are labeled with numbers 1, 3, 5, and 7, with appropriate flats for minor or diminished intervals and sharps for augmented intervals above the root.
- **Available tensions** are labeled with a compound interval number and the letter T for tension—T9, T11, T13—with appropriate flats for minor intervals

and sharps for augmented intervals above the root. The rules for availability depend on the nature of the chord, as described previously.

- **Harmonic avoid notes** are labeled with a small interval number and the letter s (for scale degree)—s2, s4, s6—with appropriate flats for minor intervals and sharps for augmented intervals above the root. These pitches may be included in the melody and often carry the unique character of each individual scale. They should not be sustained, appear on strong beats, or included in chord voicings.

CHORD SCALES FOR DIATONIC CHORDS IN MAJOR

Chord scales associated with diatonic chords in major use names inherited by the modes of Greek antiquity—Ionian, Dorian, Phrygian, Lydian, Mixolydian, Aeolian, and Locrian—although, they do not match the actual modes used at that time. In order to use the chord scale theory effectively, it is imperative to have a fluent understanding of each individual mode:

- whether it is major or minor (based on the third scale degree)
- its *characteristic pitch*—the note that makes the mode unique compared to its parallel major or minor scale

It is also important to memorize the order in which they appear relative to the major scale.

MODAL HARMONY VS. MODES IN FUNCTIONAL HARMONY

We are not exploring modal harmony here; that will be the focus of the last section of this book. Now, we are using the names of the modes to describe the chord scales that match the diatonic chords in a major key.

95

The *Ionian* mode is identical (for our purposes) to the major scale. The characteristic pitch is natural 4.

FIG. 21.2. C Ionian

96
The *Dorian* mode can be derived from the major scale by starting on the second degree (Re) and playing the seven diatonic notes up from there. It is a minor mode with natural 6 and ♭7 scale degrees. The characteristic pitch is natural 6.

1 2 ♭3 4 5 6 ♭7 1

FIG. 21.3. D Dorian

 97
The *Phrygian* mode can be derived from the major scale by starting on the third scale degree (Mi) and playing the seven diatonic notes from there. It is a minor mode with a ♭2 scale degree. The characteristic pitch is ♭2.

1 ♭2 ♭3 4 5 ♭6 ♭7 1

FIG. 21.4. E Phrygian

 98
The *Lydian* mode can be derived from the major scale by starting on the fourth scale degree (Fa) and playing the seven diatonic notes from there. It is a major mode with a ♯4 scale degree. The characteristic pitch is ♯4.

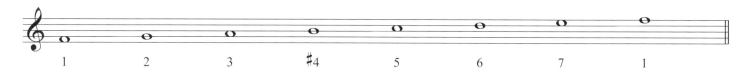

1 2 3 ♯4 5 6 7 1

FIG. 21.5. F Lydian

 99
The *Mixolydian* mode can be derived from the major scale by starting on the fifth scale degree (Sol) and playing the seven diatonic notes from there. It is a major mode with a ♭7 scale degree. The characteristic pitch is ♭7.

1 2 3 4 5 6 ♭7 1

FIG. 21.6. G Mixolydian

The *Aeolian* mode can be derived from the major scale by starting on the sixth scale degree (La). It is identical to the natural minor scale. The characteristic pitch is ♭6.

FIG. 21.7. A Aeolian

The *Locrian* mode can be derived from the major scale by starting on the seventh scale degree (Ti) and playing the seven diatonic notes from there. It is a minor mode with a ♭2 and ♭5 scale degrees. The characteristic pitches are ♭2 and ♭5.

FIG. 21.8. B Locrian

DRILL CORNER

1. Memorize the order in which modes appear relative to major: Ionian, Dorian, Phrygian, Lydian, Mixolydian, Aeolian, Locrian.

2. Memorize which of the modes are major and which minor, as well as the characteristic pitch for each mode.

Mode	Quality	Characteristic Note
Ionian	Major	natural 4
Dorian	Minor	natural 6
Phrygian	Minor	flat 2
Lydian	Major	sharp 4
Mixolydian	Major	flat 7
Aeolian	Minor	flat 6
Locrian	Minor	flat 2 and flat 5

INSTRUMENT ASSIGNMENT

1. Play all seven modes *relative* to a key signature. Try this in every key.

2. Play all seven modes *parallel*, starting on the same *Do*. Sing along in solfège, numbers, and letters.

 ASSIGNMENT 21.1

CHORD SCALES ASSOCIATED WITH DIATONIC CHORDS

Now that we are familiar with the characteristic pitch of each mode, as well as the order in which they appear when derived from the major scale, we can match each diatonic chord to each chord scale as follows (demonstrated in the key of C major):

Ionian (Chord Scale for Imaj7)

Imaj7
Cmaj7

1 — T9 — 3 — s4 — 5 — T13 — 7 — 1

Dorian (Chord Scale for IImin7)

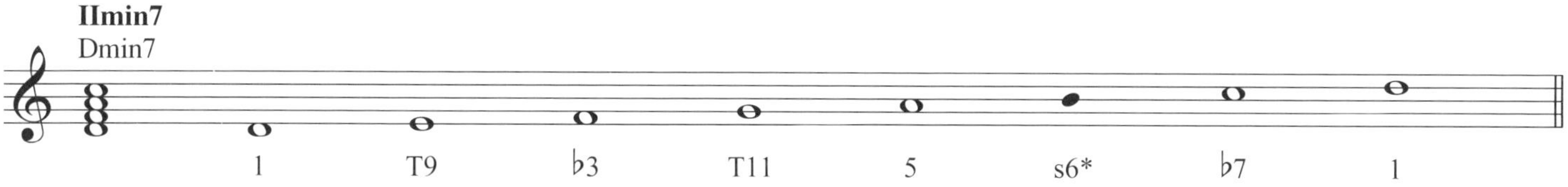

IImin7
Dmin7

1 — T9 — ♭3 — T11 — 5 — s6* — ♭7 — 1

Phrygian (Chord Scale for IIImin7)

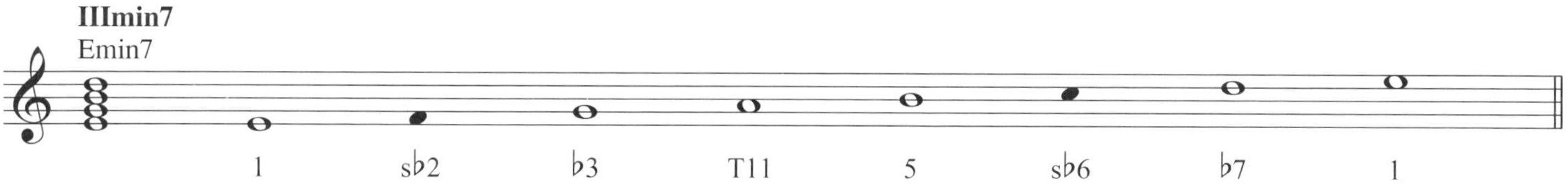

IIImin7
Emin7

1 — s♭2 — ♭3 — T11 — 5 — s♭6 — ♭7 — 1

Lydian (Chord Scale for IV7)

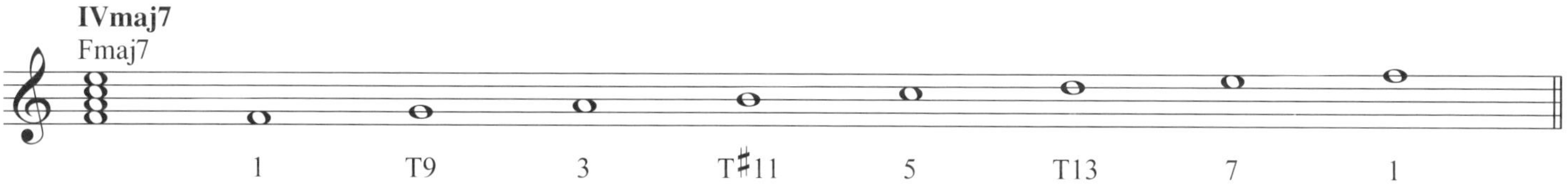

IVmaj7
Fmaj7

1 — T9 — 3 — T♯11 — 5 — T13 — 7 — 1

Mixolydian (Chord Scale for V7)

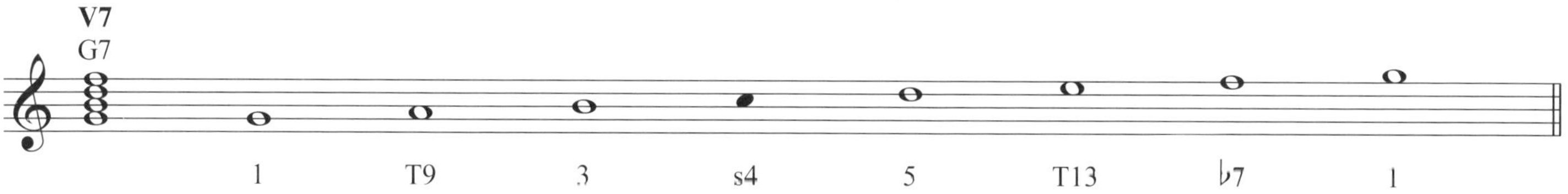

V7
G7

1 — T9 — 3 — s4 — 5 — T13 — ♭7 — 1

Aeolian (Chord Scale for VImin7)

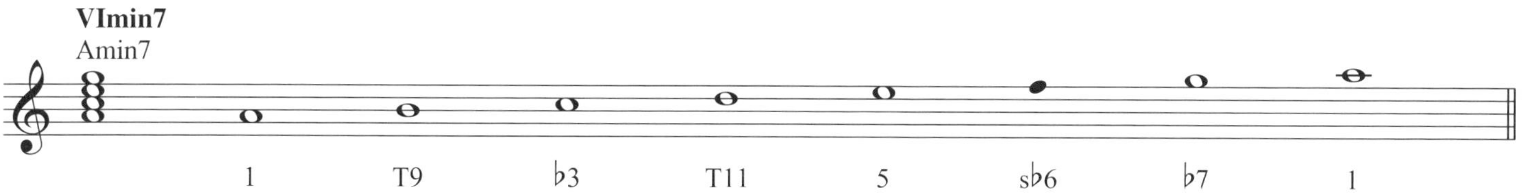

VImin7
Amin7

1 — T9 — ♭3 — T11 — 5 — s♭6 — ♭7 — 1

Locrian (Chord Scale for VIImin7♭5)

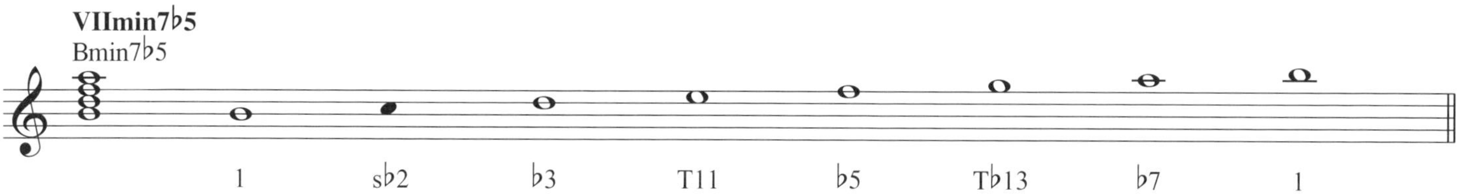

VIImin7♭5
Bmin7♭5

1 — s♭2 — ♭3 — T11 — ♭5 — T♭13 — ♭7 — 1

FIG. 21.9. Chord Scales

---

* Dorian, s6/note B: Although the 6 is a major second above the 5, it is considered an avoid note on a IImin7 chord because it creates the dominant tritone of the key when combined with the ♭3 of the IImin7 chord, resulting in a sound that is similar to the dominant chord of the key in second inversion. Since the role of the IImin7 chord is to support the dominant, not steal its power, we tend to avoid playing that tension in the voicing of a chord.

CHORD SCALES FOR DIATONIC CHORDS IN MINOR

When we stay diatonic to natural minor, chord scales follow the same logic as chord scales in major. The chord scale attached to the Imin7 chord is Aeolian, IImin7♭5 takes Locrian, ♭IIImaj7 takes Ionian, and so on.

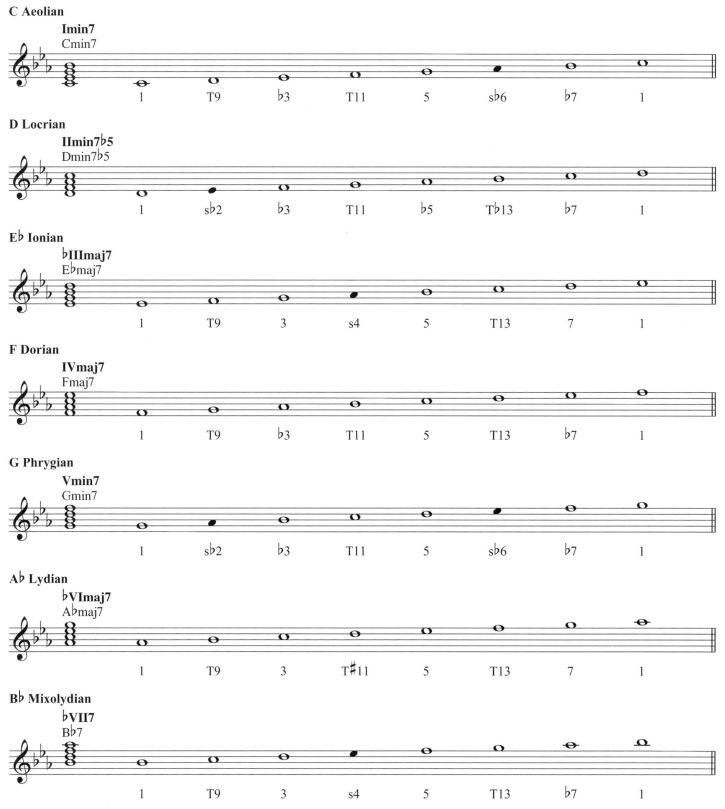

FIG. 21.10. Chord Scales in C Natural Minor

As you may expect, things get a bit more interesting when we look at chord scales using compound minor as source material. Here are some of the more common chord scales associated with chords in compound minor.

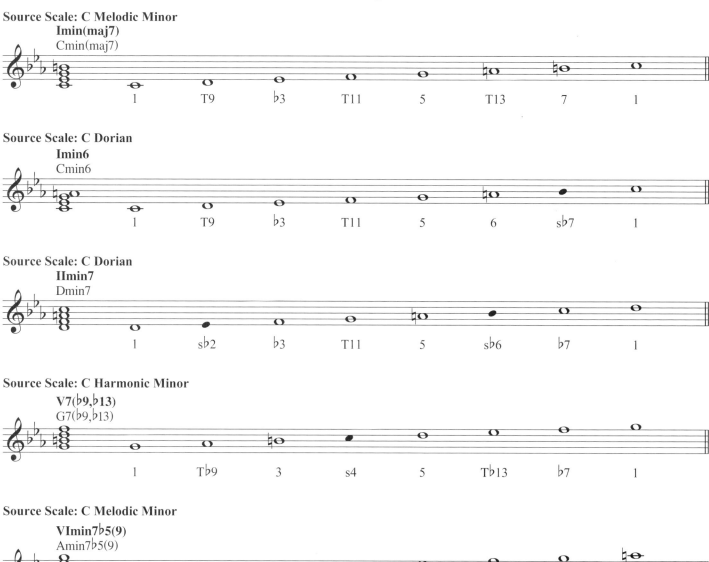

FIG. 21.11. Chord Scales in Compound Minor

CHORD SCALES FOR SECONDARY DOMINANTS

All dominant chords use a version of the Mixolydian mode, since it is the only mode that contains a major 3 and a minor 7—the two components crucial to the structure of a dominant chord. However, since tensions on secondary dominant chords vary depending on the quality of the target chord, the chord scale for each secondary dominant chord needs to reflect that.

If the chord of resolution has a major 3rd (V7/IV and V7/V), the chord scale associated with the secondary dominant is Mixolydian.

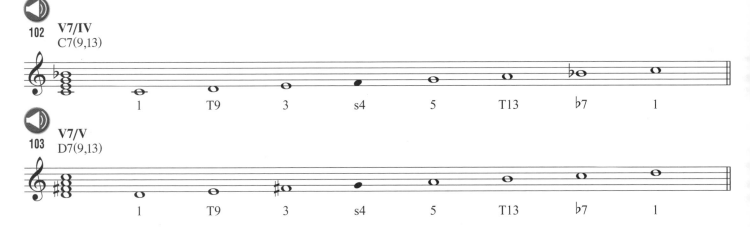

FIG. 21.12. Chord Scale for Secondary Dominants Resolving to a Major 3rd

If the chord of resolution has a minor 3rd (V7/III and V7/VI), the chord scale associated with the dominant chord is Mixolydian ♭9, ♯9, ♭13.

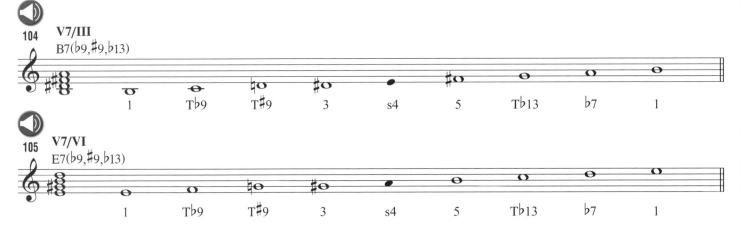

FIG. 21.13. Chord Scale for Secondary Dominants Resolving to a Minor 3rd

In the case of V7/II, the diatonic tensions suggest Mixolydian ♭13, although in practice, the Mixolydian ♭9, ♯9, ♭13 is often used.

FIG. 21.14. Chord Scale for A7 as V7/II

TENSIONS ON SECONDARY DOMINANTS ARE DIATONIC

When building chord scales for secondary dominants, it is useful to remember that tensions on secondary dominants are *diatonic to the key of the piece.*

The expressive potential of the dominant chord may be further enhanced by altering some or all of the tensions, as well as the otherwise natural 5 of the chord. The following scales may be used when more tension is desired, or when the 5th of the chord is either lowered or raised to a ♭5 or ♯5, respectively.

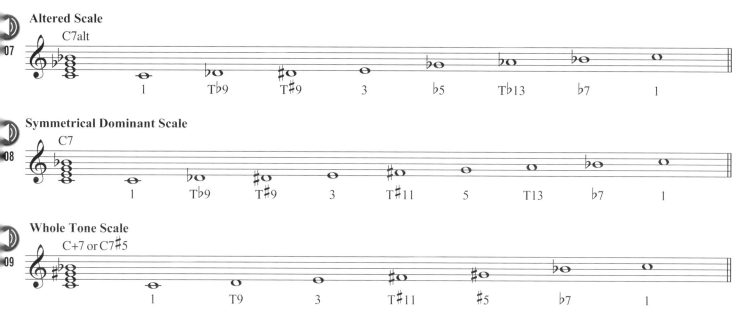

FIG. 21.15. Scales for Added Tension: Altered, Symmetrical Dominant, Whole Tone

CHORD SCALES FOR RELATED II CHORDS

Related II chords are either min7 or min7♭5 in quality. Furthermore, they fall into two categories: diatonic to the key (dual function), and non-diatonic related II.

All min7♭5 related II chords use Locrian.

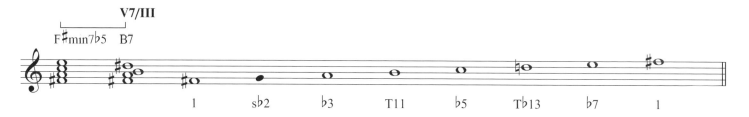

FIG. 21.16. Chord Scale for F♯min7♭5 as a Related II Chord to B7 in the Key of C Major

All non-diatonic min7 related II chords use Dorian, avoiding s6 in order to avoid the undesired dominant effect it creates with the ♭3 of the chord as discussed earlier.

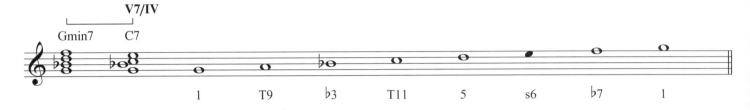

FIG. 21.17. Chord Scale for Gmin7 as Related II Chord to C7 in the Key of C Major

Related II chords with dual function may use the chord scale diatonic to the key, or Dorian. The choice is often implied by the melody. In some cases, it is a matter of personal preference or style.

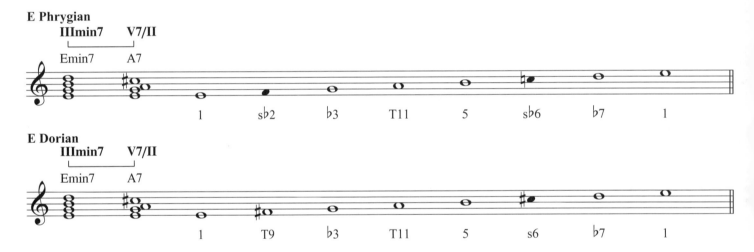

FIG. 21.18. A Choice of Chord Scales for Emin7: Phrygian or Dorian

CHORD SCALES FOR SUBSTITUTE DOMINANTS

As you recall from chapter 19, substitute dominants are dominant chords built a tritone away from the original dominant chord they are substituting for. Any of the five secondary dominants, as well as the primary dominant of the key, may be replaced or enhanced by the use of a substitute dominant.

Since substitute dominants are a far departure from the diatonic pitches of the key, their tensions are not diatonic either. Rather, each tension is a whole step above the chord tone below it. The resulting scale is Lydian ♭7, and the tensions associated with substitute dominants are 9, #11, and 13.

110

FIG. 21.19. C Lydian ♭7

Another way to look at the Lydian ♭7 scale can be found in its relationship to the altered scale we introduced earlier in this chapter. Since the substitute dominant is built a tritone away from the original dominant chord, we can build a new scale starting on the ♭5 of the C altered scale. The result is G♭ Lydian ♭7. The two scales are relative to each other.

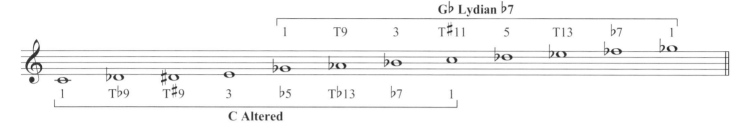

FIG. 21.20. C Altered and G♭ Lydian ♭7 as Chord Scales for C7alt and G♭7 Respectively

Note: the D♯ and E are spelled enharmonically as E♭ and F♭ respectively in the upper octave.

CHORD SCALES FOR MODAL INTERCHANGE CHORDS

Modal interchange chords present a delightful opportunity to alter the mood of a piece, while enriching the chromatic possibilities for both harmony and melody. The choice of chord scales associated with modal interchange chords depends on style and personal interpretation, while it is closely linked to the source or parallel mode the chord has been borrowed from. For example, if the IV7 chord is borrowed from the parallel melodic minor, the chord scale it takes is Lydian ♭7, while the same IV7 chord borrowed from the parallel Dorian will yield the use of Mixolydian.

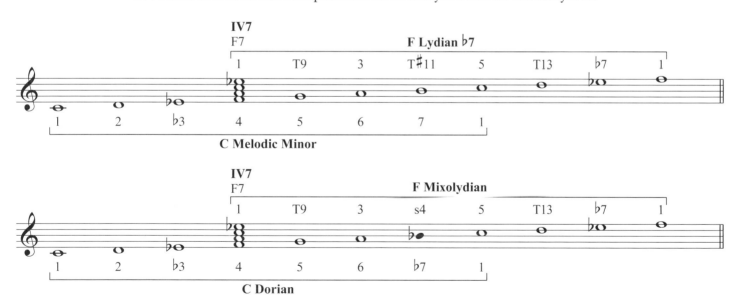

FIG. 21.21. Chord Scales for F7 as a Modal Interchange Chord in the Key of C Major

In addition to the source of the chord, the major context of the main key of the piece may also influence the implied chord scale by asserting its own major 3 and replacing the minor 3 of the parallel minor.

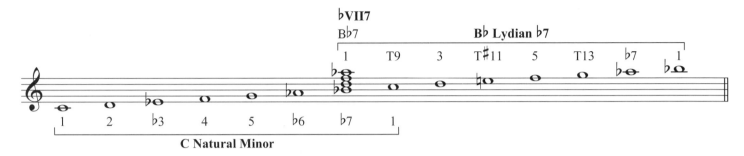

FIG. 21.22. Chord Scale for B♭7 as a Modal Interchange Chord in C Major

As a result, the choices may become overwhelming. However, in practice, modal interchange chords fall under the following rule of thumb:

- Major 7 M.I. chords (such as ♭IImaj7, ♭IIImaj7, ♭VImaj7, ♭VIImaj7) use Lydian.
- Minor 7 M.I. chords (such as Imin7 and IVmin7) use Dorian with no avoid notes.
- Dominant 7 M.I. chords (such as IV7 and ♭VII7) use Lydian ♭7.
- Minor7♭5 M.I. chords (such as IImin7♭5 and VImin7♭5) use Locrian or Locrian with a natural 9.

CHAPTER 22

Diminished Chords and Chord Scales

The fully diminished chord is unique both in structure and function. Built by stacking three minor thirds, the structure of the diminished chord contains not one but two tritones, rendering it very unstable and prone to quick resolution.

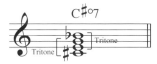

FIG. 22.1. Tritones in a Diminished Chord

When spelling fully diminished chords, we often use enharmonic spelling in order to avoid awkward accidentals.

FIG. 22.2. Enharmonic Spelling of Diminished Chords

Although a fully diminished chord may be built on the leading tone of harmonic minor, in practice, we encounter this structure much more often in the context of a **major key** in one of the following roles:

1. **Ascending:** as the upper structure (3, 5, ♭7, and ♭9) of a secondary dominant, resolving upwards

2. **Descending:** as a passing or approaching chord moving downwards

3. **Auxiliary:** as an embellishing chord to the I or V of the key

ASCENDING DIMINISHED SEVENTH CHORD: SECONDARY DOMINANT FUNCTION

Play the example in figure 22.3, and listen closely to the familiar sense of resolution.

FIG. 22.3. V7/III Resolving to IIImin7 in the Key of C Major

Now compare that to the following cadence:

FIG. 22.4. #II°7 Moving Up to IIImin7 in the Key of C Major

Looking closely at the notes of the B7(♭9) in figure 22.3, you see that the 3, 5, ♭7 and ♭9 of B7 spell out D♯°7. Moreover, the tritone between D♯ and A resolves to E and G respectively, exactly the way they did in the B7 to Emin7 resolution in figure 22.3. The Roman numeral for D♯°7 reflects the scale degree it is built on, namely #II, and the choice of D♯ vs. E♭ reflects the ascending motion of the chord.

A similar pattern emerges with #I°7, #IV°7, and #V°7 standing in for V7/II, V7/V, and V7/VI respectively.

- **#I°7.** "Wrong Places" by H.E.R. From *Songland* (TV show), Episode 3, 2020. "For Once in My Life" by Stevie Wonder. (Ron Miller, Orlando Murden) Stevie Wonder, *For Once in My Life*, Motown Records, 1968.
- **#V° resolving up to the VImin chord.** "Blackbird" by Lennon/McCartney. The Beatles, *The White Album*, Apple, 1968.
- **#V° resolving up to the VImin chord.** "First Love Late Spring" by Mitski. *Bury Me at Makeout Creek*, Double Double Whammy Don Giovanni Records, 2014.

FIG. 22.5. Chord Progression Using #V° Ascending Up to VImin

The chord scale associated with ascending diminished chords follows the same logic as secondary dominants. We fill in the spaces between the chord tones with notes diatonic to the key. Another practical way to look at that is interlocking the chord tones of the diminished chord with the chord tone of the resolution:

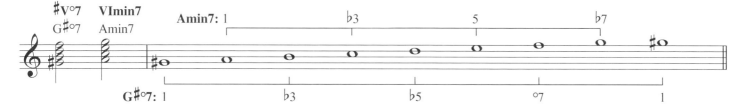

FIG. 22.6. Combining Chord Tones for G#°7 and Amin7 into One Scale

As was the case with tensions on diatonic chords, notes that sit a whole step above the chord tone below are available, while notes that sit a half step above are considered avoid notes. Unlike chord scales on all other chords, the convention for diminished chord scales is to leave the avoid notes without a scale degree number as to avoid the complication of enharmonic spellings and awkward intervals. One more notable difference is tension 7, which appears between the diminished 7 of the chord and the root doubled at the octave.

FIG. 22.7. Chord Scale for G#°7 as #V°7 in the Key of C Major

Since G#°7 plays a similar role as E7 as V7/VI, the relationship between the two chords can be seen once again in the overlapping of the two scales: simply begin the chord scale for G#°7 on the 3 of E Mixolydian (♭9, #9, ♭13).

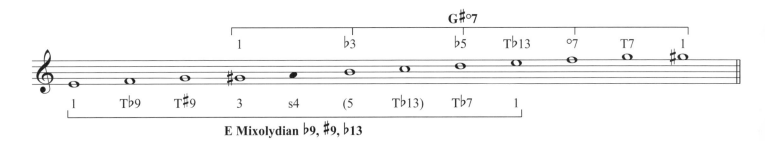

FIG. 22.8. Chord Scale for G#°7

All ascending diminished chords can have an alternative resolution that could be heard in popular repertoire.

FIG. 22.9. Alternative Resolution of Ascending Diminished Chords

DESCENDING DIMINISHED CHORDS: PASSING OR APPROACH CHORDS

On the surface, the descending diminished chords appear similar to the ascending ones, only moving down (instead of up) by half step into the next chord. The big difference is that there is no actual tritone resolution here. The diminished chord simply passes between two diatonic chords (passing descending) or approaches a diatonic chord by half step from above (approach descending).

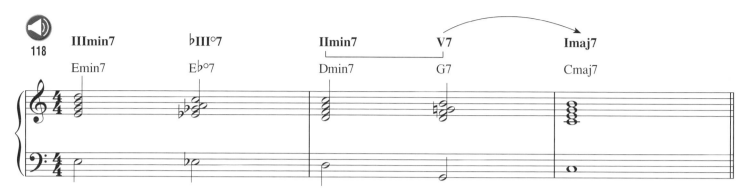

FIG. 22.10. ♭III°7 Descending into IImin7 in the Key of C Major

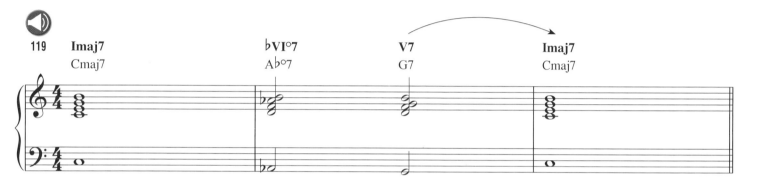

FIG. 22.11. ♭VI°7 Descending into V7 in the Key of C Major

Once again, the choice to use E♭ vs. D♯ and A♭ vs. G♯ reflects the downward motion of the progression. The chord scales for these chords are identical to their ascending counterparts, spelled enharmonically.

FIG. 22.12. Chord Scale for E♭°7 as a Descending ♭III°7 in the Key of C Major

Descending diminished chords may also have a possible alternative resolution as follows:

FIG. 22.13. Alternative Resolution for Descending Diminished Chords

AUXILIARY DIMINISHED CHORDS: EMBELLISHING THE I AND V

The last category of diminished chords are the I°7 and the V°7. They may appear sandwiched between two Imaj7 or V7 chords respectively:

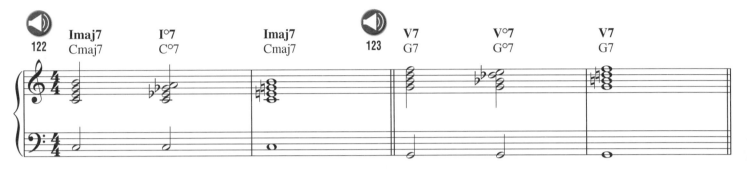

FIG. 22.14. Auxiliary Diminished Chords

This creates the effect of harmonic motion without change of function or root.

The I°7 may also appear as a delayed resolution at the end of a cadence:

FIG. 22.15. I°7 as Delayed Resolution

The chord scales for both auxiliary diminished chords follows the same logic: chord tones interlaced with notes diatonic to the key.

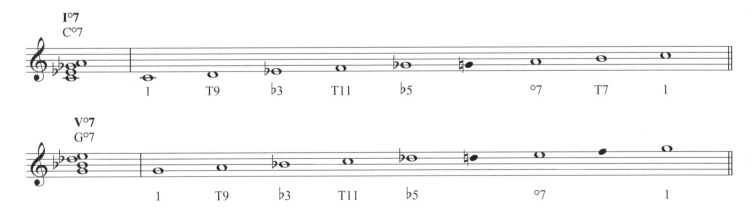

FIG. 22.16. Chord Scales for I°7 and V°7 in the Key of C Major

With the ever-insatiable desire of contemporary musicians to invite more outside notes into their improvisation, another alternative chord scale for diminished chords has entered the vocabulary: the symmetrical diminished scale. Here, all four tensions are a whole step above the chord tone below, making them available, regardless of whether the pitch is diatonic to the key or not. In fact, this scale is not diatonic to any key, but may be used any time a more surprising effect is desired.

FIG. 22.17. C Symmetrical Diminished Scale

The notes of the symmetrical diminished scale create an even pattern of whole steps alternating with half steps. Similarly, the symmetrical dominant scale introduced in chapter 21 follows the reverse pattern of half step followed by a whole step. As a result, some musicians refer to the symmetrical diminished scale as "whole-half" and the symmetrical dominant scale as "half-whole."

CHAPTER 23

Modulation

A *modulation* occurs when both the melody and harmony of a tune move to a new key long enough that our perception of the original tonal center Do shifts to a new pitch. If Do remains the same, but the mode changes—for example from major to minor—we have change of mode, rather than modulation to a new key. And if the key changes very briefly but returns to the original key before the new key has been fully established, we have *tonicization*, or key of the moment.

A modulation may occur between closely related keys—ones that share a lot of common pitches, and between distantly related keys—ones that share very few common pitches, or none. A good way to judge whether two keys are closely or distantly related is by looking at how closely they sit in the circle of fifths. The closer they are in the circle, the more pitches they share. Finally, a modulation may occur between two major keys, two minor keys, or a major and a minor key.

There are three common ways to modulate:

1. **directly**—switching key without a warning

2. by using a **pivot chord** or cadence—one that functions in both the old and the new key

3. by using a **transitional passage**—a series of chords that obliterate the sense of the old key and eventually establish a new one

Each method comes with its advantages and challenges, and each method has a purpose and carries an emotional impact on the listener. Let's explore the three kinds of modulation.

DIRECT MODULATION

As the name implies, a *direct modulation* occurs when the key changes abruptly to a new one. As a compositional device, this modulation is often used to create a welcome surprise on the bridge of a tune, as you may hear in songs like "Prelude to a Kiss," "Body and Soul," "New York State of Mind," "You Are the Sunshine of My Life," and numerous others.

- "Prelude to a Kiss" by Duke Ellington, Irving Mills, Irving Gordon. Billie Holiday, *Velvet Mood,* Verve MG V-8096, 1955.
- "Body and Soul" by Johnny Green, Edward Heyman, Robert Sour, Frank Eyton. Tony Bennett and Amy Winehouse, *Duets II,* Columbia, 2011.
- "New York State of Mind" by Billy Joel. *Turnstiles,* Family Productions/ Columbia, 1976.
- "You Are the Sunshine of My Life" by Stevie Wonder. *Talking Book,* Tamla Motown, 1972.

As an arranging tool, you will find direct modulations in the final tag of a tune, harmonizing a melodic sequence of the hook of the song, such as in "Golden Lady" by Stevie Wonder.*

In pop music, direct modulation is often used to create excitement to an otherwise simple progression, as is the case in "The Way You Love Me" by Faith Hill.**

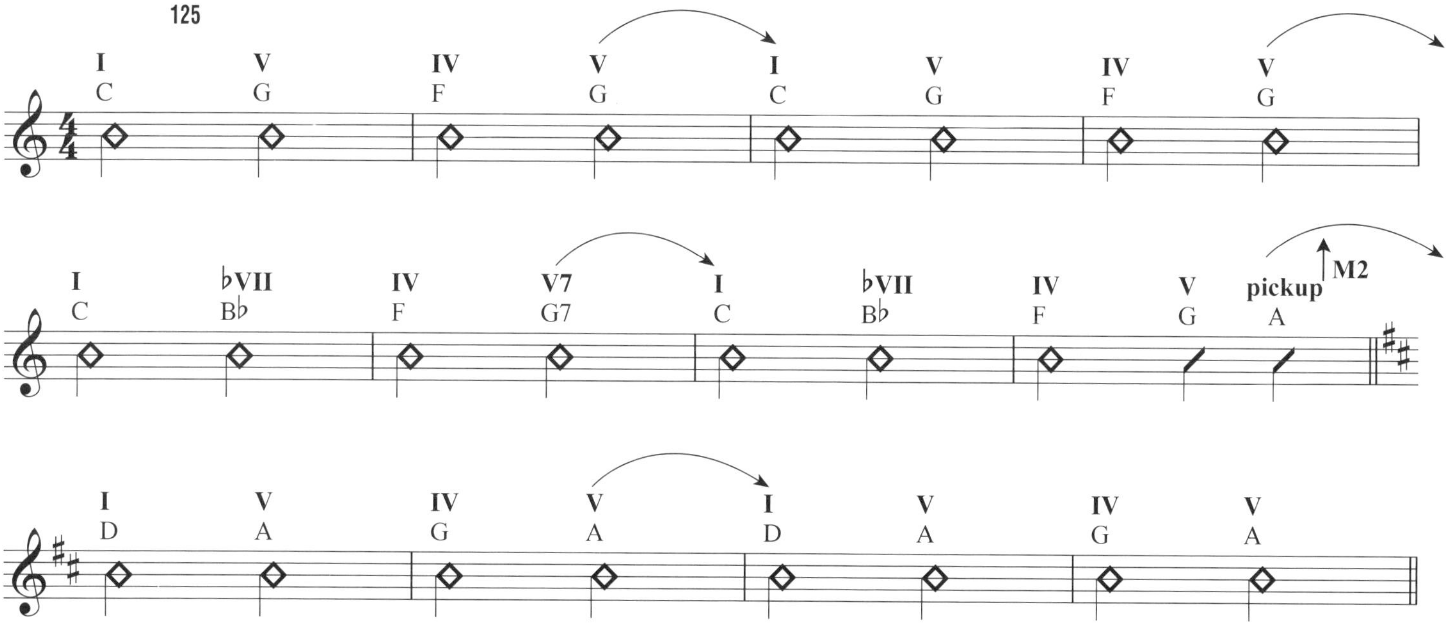

FIG. 23.1. Direct Modulation

PIVOT MODULATION

A *pivot modulation* occurs when a chord (or often two chords) functions in both the old and the new key. Secondary dominants, substitute dominants, and modal interchange chords are great candidates for pivot modulation, since they function in more than one key.

---

* Stevie Wonder, *Innervisions,* Tamla Motown, 1973.
** Written by Michael Dulaney and Keith Follese. Faith Hill, *Breathe,* Warner Brothers, 1999.

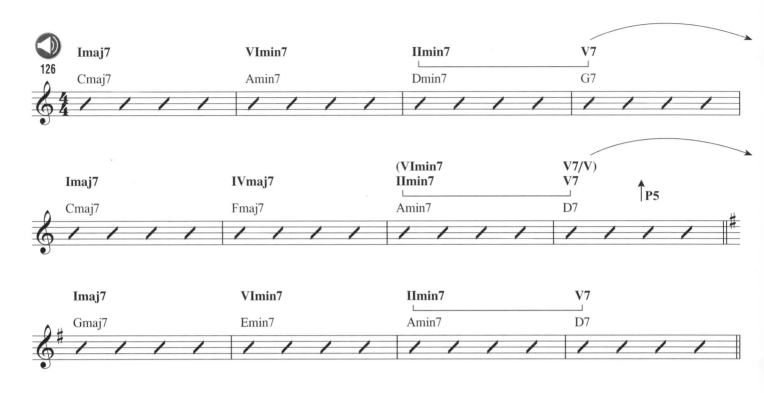

FIG. 23.2. Pivot Modulation Using a II V Pair Functional in Both Keys

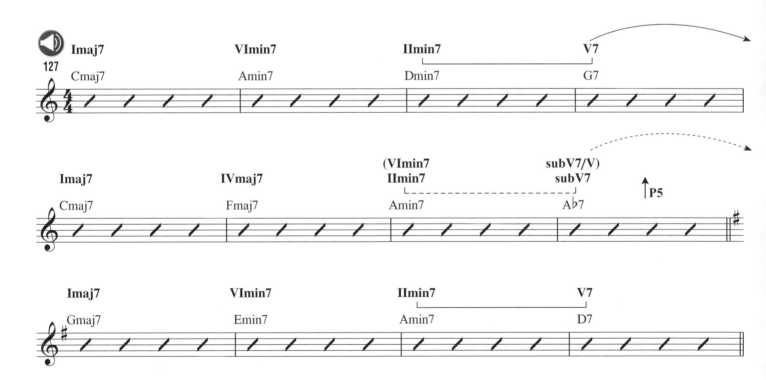

FIG. 23.3. Typical Substitute Dominant IImin7 subV7 Pivot Modulation

Here are some great examples of a pivot modulation using a IImin7 V7 cadence as either secondary or substitute dominants:

- **V7/VI becomes V7 in the new key; ♭VII7 becomes the V7 in the original key.** "You Are the Sunshine of My Life" by Stevie Wonder. *Talking Book*, Tamla Motown, 1972.

- **V7/V becomes the V7 of the new key.** "Everlasting Love" by Buzz Cason and Mac Gayden. Robert Knight, *Everlasting Love*, Rising Sons (RS45-705), 1967.
- **V7/IV becomes V7 of the new key.** "Kodachrome," by Paul Simon. *There Goes Rhymin' Simon*, Columbia, 1973.

Modal interchange chords are good candidates for pivot modulation. A typical pivot modal interchange chord is the ♭VII7, often in combination with IVmin7. The two chords appear as modal interchange in the original key, then become a IImin7 V7 in the new key.

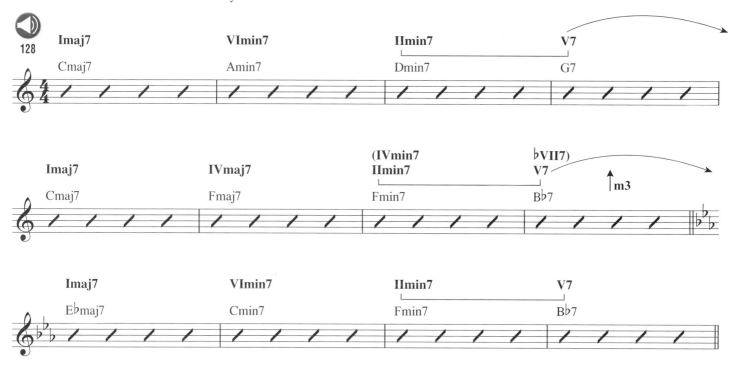

FIG. 23.4. Typical IVmin7 ♭VII7 Pivot Modulation

Here are some examples of a ♭VII7 chord used as pivot:

- **Pivot ♭VII7 at the end of the chorus becomes the V7 of the bridge.** "You're Gonna Lose That Girl" by the Beatles. Lennon/McCartney. The Beatles, *Help!*, Parlophone, 1965.
- **At the end of the chorus, pivot IV becomes the new ♭VII going back to the verse.** "Come in with the Rain," Taylor Swift. *Fearless*, Big Machine, 2008.

TRANSITIONAL MODULATION

Aptly named, a transitional modulation employs a series of chords that do not belong to any one key in particular, such as extended dominants, extended substitute dominants, constant structure, contiguous dominants (see chapter 26), or any free-composed progression that does not neatly fit within a key. The result is a gradual loss of a sense of key, an exciting tonally ambiguous period, and finally the establishment of a new key.

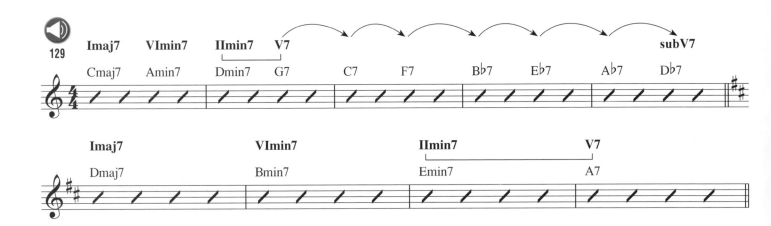

FIG. 23.5. Transitional Modulation

Two great examples of a transitional modulation are "Lately" and "You Are the Sunshine of My Life" by Stevie Wonder.

Many songs use multiple modulation techniques. Listen to:

- "Body and Soul" by Johnny Mercer and Edward Heyman. Tony Bennett and Amy Winehouse, *Duets II,* Columbia, 2011.
- "You Are the Sunshine of My Life" by Stevie Wonder. Stevie Wonder, *Talking Book,* Tamla Motown, 1972.
- "Early Autumn" by Johnny Mercer, Woody Herman. Woody Herman and His Orchestra, *Capitol Jazz Classics, Vol. 9*, Capitol Records, M-11034, 1972.

Blues Reharmonization

In chapter 13, we introduced the blues as one of the most ubiquitous chord progression, genre, style, and form. As jazz harmony was becoming more complicated and sophisticated, jazz musicians turned to the blues with fresh eyes, and began reharmonizing the basic chord progression. The process of reharmonizing involves changing or adding chords to an existing chord progression, while keeping the main structure and essence intact.

In this chapter, we will explore some of the most common blues "reharm" gestures historically found during the bebop era. There are many more possibilities out there, which you are welcome to explore on your own. Just remember, the more chords you change and add, the further away from the traditional blues form you will be.

31

As a reminder, here is a basic blues progression, including a quick change in the second measure:

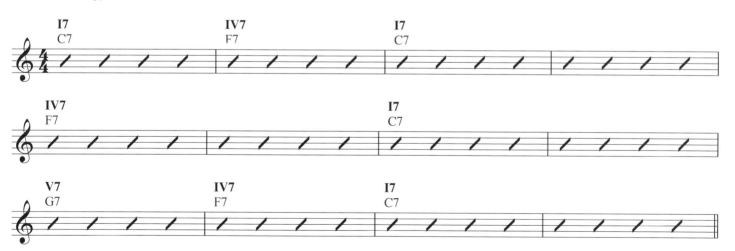

FIG. 24.1. Basic Blues Progression with a Quick Change to the IV7 Chord

130

The most common blues reharm gesture is to use secondary dominants, usually with their related II chords. The end of a phrase is a good place for that.

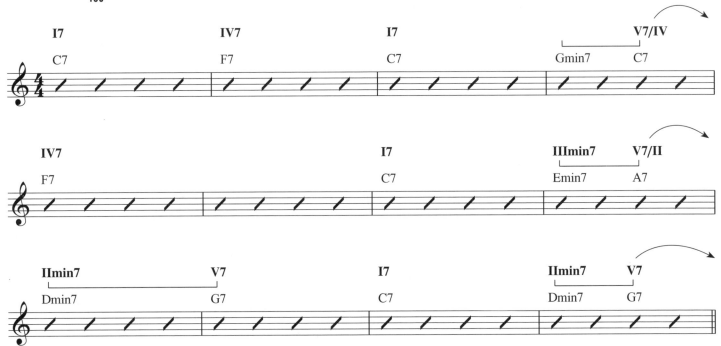

FIG. 24.2. Secondary Dominants in Blues Reharmonization

Notice the change in measures 9 and 10. Rather than adding a chord to measure 9 to create a II V pair, we usually spread the pair over two measures.

Next, add a passing diminished chord ♯IV°7 in measure 6 that links the IV7 chord in measure 5 and the I7 chord in measure 7. It is common to invert the I7 chord in measure 7 to I7/5, C7/G. That gesture creates a smooth chromatic bass line: F, F♯, G.

Finally, we add a typical turnaround in measures 11 and 12 using I VI II V. You will often find the VImin7 chord converted to a dominant structure, thus creating a V7/II resolving to the IImin7 chord and creating forward momentum.

131

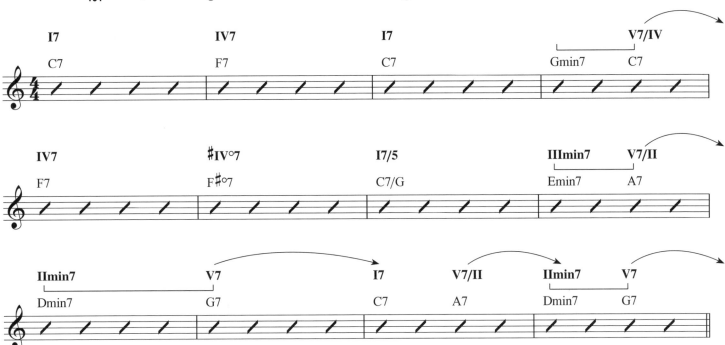

FIG. 24.3. Complete Blues Reharmonization

There is one more notable example of blues reharmonization, the so-called "Bird Blues" or "Parker Blues," named after Charlie Parker, who uses it in his famous standard "Blues for Alice."*

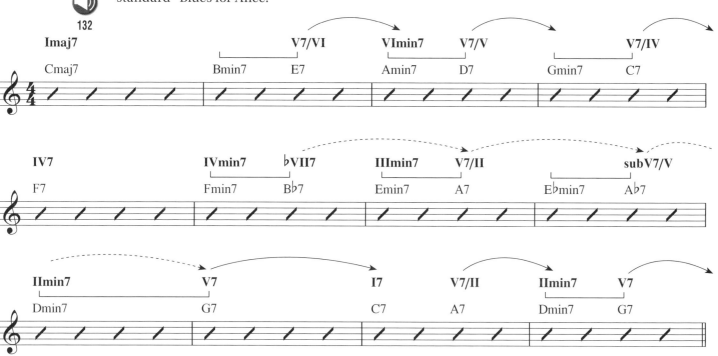

FIG. 24.4. Bird Blues

The Bird Blues forgoes the use of dominant structure and starts on a Imaj7, thus establishing a more modern jazz sound from the start. Measures 2, 3, and 4 use a pattern of cycling secondary dominants and their related II chords, targeting the IV7 chord in measure 5, thus preserving the blues nature of the chord progression. Measures 6, 7, and 8 utilize a similar pattern of cycling substitute dominants with interpolated related II chords, eventually resolving to the V7 chord in measure 10. The turnaround in measures 11 and 12 is the same as before.

As you can see, there are many options when reharmonizing the blues. You can mix and match any of these variations and of course, you can come up with your own version of blues reharmonization as long as you keep the main elements in place: the I chord in measure 1, the IV chord in measure 5, and some type of a turnaround in measures 9 and 10.

---

* Charlie Parker, *The Complete Charlie Parker on Verve,* Verve, 1990.

CHAPTER 25

Advanced Chord Voicings: Polychords; Hybrid Chords

In chapter 12, we introduced some basic chord voicings for comping instruments, utilizing the most important notes of a chord: 3 and 7, against a root played either by the left hand on the piano or a separate bass player. We also looked at tension substitution, whereby the doubled root of the chord is replaced by tension 9, while the expendable fifth is replaced by tension 13.

In this chapter, we'll address a few more contemporary chord voicings that may be used as a songwriting, composition, or arranging tool, whether we are writing for a solo piano player, a small ensemble, a big band, a full orchestra, or any other group.

POLYCHORDS

As the name suggests, a *polychord* consists of two seemingly unrelated chords—an upper and a lower structure—that when played together produce the effect of a single chord with tensions.

$$\frac{\text{G}}{\text{Cmaj7}} = \text{Cmaj7(9)}$$

The *lower structure* of the polychord consists of the root, third, and seventh. It is always in root position, while the 3 and 7 may be voiced open or closed. The function and Roman numeral (and therefore the implied chord scale associated with the chord) are based entirely on the lower structure of the polychord. The *upper structure* contains available tensions, and may repeat any chord tones, with the exception of the root on major seventh chords.

Constructing polychords is easy, as long as you know the chord scale associated with the lower structure and the available tensions and avoid notes. You also need to be able to construct triads and seventh chords outside of a given key.

FIG. 25.1. Possible Polychords for Cmaj7 Using C Ionian

Figure 25.1 shows that $\dfrac{\text{G}}{\text{Cmaj7}}$ is the best available option for a polychord on a Cmaj7.

Although the Emin7 does not contain either the root or the avoid note of C Ionian, it does not create an effective upper structure for a Cmaj7 polychord since it doubles three chord tones and only adds one tension. Generally speaking, the best scale degrees to build an upper structure on are 2, 5, and 7.

FIG. 25.2. Possible Polychords for Fmaj7 Using F Lydian

FIG. 25.3. Possible Polychords for G7 Using G Mixolydian

Note: Phrygian and Locrian modes do not produce any effective polychords.

Best practices when constructing a polychord:
- Keep the upper and lower structures at least a minor third away from each other.
- Avoid doubling the root, especially on major seventh chords.
- Build the upper structure starting on the second, fifth, or seventh scale degree of the chord scale associated with the lower structure.

Here is a reference sheet for the most commonly used polychords by chord scale. The upper structure is represented here by a Roman numeral based on the scale degree it is built on, while R stands for the chord in the lower structure.

Polychords Per Chord Scale

Scale	Polychords
Ionian	$\dfrac{V}{R}$ Example for C Ionian: $\dfrac{G}{Cmaj7}$
Dorian	$\dfrac{IImin}{R^*}$ $\dfrac{Vmin}{R}$ $\dfrac{Vmin7}{R}$ $\dfrac{\flat VII}{R}$ $\dfrac{\flat VIImaj7}{R^*}$
Lydian	$\dfrac{II}{R}$ $\dfrac{V}{R}$ $\dfrac{Vmaj7}{R}$ $\dfrac{VIImin}{R}$ $\dfrac{VIImin7}{R}$
Mixolydian	$\dfrac{Vmin}{R}$
Aeolian	$\dfrac{Vmin}{R}$ $\dfrac{Vmin7}{R}$ $\dfrac{\flat VII}{R}$
Mixolydian ♭9, ♯9, ♭13	$\dfrac{\flat IImin}{R}$ $\dfrac{\flat III}{R}$ $\dfrac{\flat III7}{R}$ $\dfrac{V^\circ}{R}$ $\dfrac{\flat VIImin7\flat5}{R}$
Lydian ♭7	$\dfrac{II}{R}$ $\dfrac{II+}{R^{**}}$ $\dfrac{Vmin}{R}$ $\dfrac{Vmin(maj)7}{R}$ $\dfrac{\flat VII+maj7}{R}$
Altered	$\dfrac{\flat IImin}{R}$ $\dfrac{\flat IIImin}{R}$ $\dfrac{\flat IIImin7}{R}$ $\dfrac{\flat V}{R}$ $\dfrac{\flat VI}{R}$ $\dfrac{\flat VI7}{R}$ $\dfrac{\flat VII^\circ}{R}$ $\dfrac{\flat VIImin7\flat5}{R}$
Phrygian and Locrian	(none)

R stands for the root of the chord.

Roman numerals relate to the root of the chord, not the key of the piece.

*Only if tension 13 is available

**Same as ♯IV+ or ♭VII+

FIG. 25.4. Most Commonly Used Polychords by Chord Scale

HYBRID CHORDS

Technically speaking, hybrid chords are more than just a voicing. They are a unique category of chords, where the third of the chord is omitted, thus creating a light, open, somewhat ambiguous sound. The voicing structure of a hybrid chord consists of a single root in the bass and a seemingly unrelated upper structure that contains available tensions and chord tones other than the third. The name and Roman numeral of the chord are based on the root note, not the upper structure.

On the surface, a hybrid chord looks a lot like an inversion, but when we examine it closely we'll see one significant difference.

FIG. 25.5. Inversion vs. Hybrid Chord

Compare G7/D vs. Dmin7/G. In the G7/D example, the base note D is part of the chord G, which makes that chord a simple inversion of the G7 over its own fifth. In the Dmin7/G example, the note G is not part of the D chord, creating a hybrid G7sus4(9).

Although all dominant 7 sus4 chords may be expressed as hybrids, not all hybrid chords are dominant 7sus4 chords!

Hybrid chords are seventh chords missing a third. They have a single bass note, as the root of the chord, and an upper structure that contains chord tones and available tensions, but not the third or the root of the chord.

When the upper structure of a hybrid chord contains the major 7th against the root, even with the 3rd missing, the implication is that the chord is a major seventh chord. Furthermore, if the upper structure contains tension #11, we can deduce that the chord is using a Lydian chord scale.

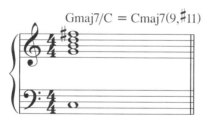

FIG. 25.6. Gmaj7/C = Cmaj7(9,#11)

Things are a bit more complicated when the upper structure contains the minor 7th against the root. In this case, the implied quality of the chord may be minor or dominant. Context, harmonic rhythm, and familiarity with the composer's style may help find the most likely analysis in this case.

Compare the Roman numeral analysis for the Emin7/A chord in the following two different contexts:

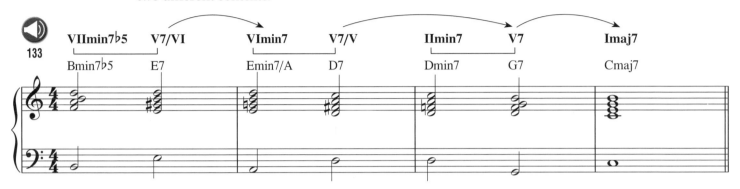

FIG. 25.7. Emin7/A as the Diatonic VImin7 in the Key of C Major

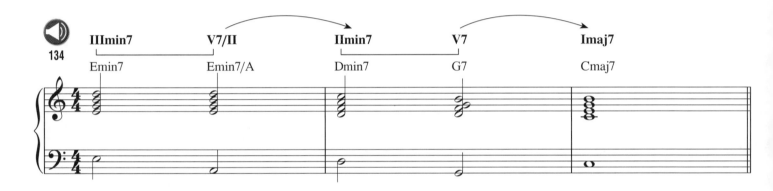

FIG. 25.8. Emin7/A as V7/II in the Key of C Major

Constructing hybrid chords is similar to constructing polychords, with one significant difference: the third of the chord scale should be avoided in the upper structure. The resulting chord for Cmaj7 is G/C.

FIG. 25.9. Hybrid Chords in C Ionian

The resulting chords for Cmaj7(♯11) are as follows:

FIG. 25.10. Hybrid Chords in C Lydian

In the case of Mixolydian, the 4th is no longer an avoid note. It may be used in the upper structure if the 7sus4 sound is desired, as shown in figure 25.5.

If the type of Mixolydian used has tensions ♭9 and ♯9, the ♯9 should be avoided because in the absence of a major 3rd it will essentially sound like a minor 3rd.

FIG. 25.11. Hybrid Chords for C Mixolydian ♭9,♯9, ♭13

When constructing hybrid chords for Dorian, we can freely use tension 13, rather than avoid it, as we did in three-way closed voicing (see chapter 21). Since the 3rd of the minor chord is not present, the 6th scale degree of the chord scale will no longer create a tritone with it, and therefore it becomes an available tension 13.

FIG. 25.12. Hybrid Chords in C Dorian

Hybrid chords are often used in modal music—the subject of the third part of this book—when the rules of what is considered an avoid note will change.

Here is a list of common hybrid chords by chord scale, similar to the one provided for polychords.

Ionian:	V/R
Dorian:	♭VII/R Vmin/R Vmin7/R ♭VIImaj7/R IImin/R
Lydian:	II/R V/R Vmaj7/R VIImin/R VIImin7/R
Mixolydian:	Vmin/R ♭VII/R ♭VIImaj7/R
Altered:	♭V/R
Mixolydian ♭9, ♭13:	♭II/R
Lydian ♭7:	II/R Vmin/R Vmin(maj)7/R ♭VIIaug/R ♭VIIaug(maj)7/R
Aeolian:	Vmin7/R ♭VII/R
MODAL ONLY	
Phrygian:	♭II/R ♭VIImin/R ♭VIImin7/R
Locrian:	♭VIImin/R ♭VIImin7/R

A few conditions when using this list:

- Do not use the modal versions in functional harmony.
- S4 in Mixolydian is allowed if you wish to create a 7sus4 sound. To create a 7sus4 sound, use ♭VII/R or ♭VIImaj7/R.
- T13 in Dorian is allowed because there is no 3rd in the chord to create a tritone with.
- Avoid T♯9 because it acts like a ♭3 in the absence of a real 3.

CHAPTER 26

Contiguous Dominants and Constant Structure

There are two more harmonic gestures worth exploring before we leave functional harmony: contiguous dominants and constant structure.

Contiguous dominants are two or more dominant chords that move up by half step, whole step, minor third, or major third. They may or may not have their related II chords with them. The tritone does not resolve; it simply moves up in parallel motion.

135

FIG. 26.1. Contiguous Dominants

136

Another use of contiguous dominants may sound like a pickup measure into the main piece.

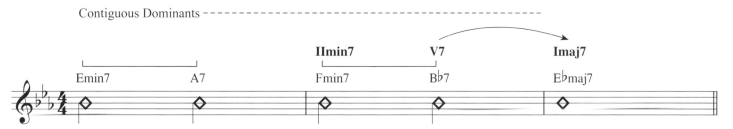

FIG. 26.2. Contiguous II V Pair

Contiguous dominants are a type of *constant structure*—that is, a chord progression composed entirely of chords of the same quality. The chords usually create a recognizable bass pattern and may not be easily analyzed with Roman numerals. Figure 26.3 demonstrates a typical constant structure.

137

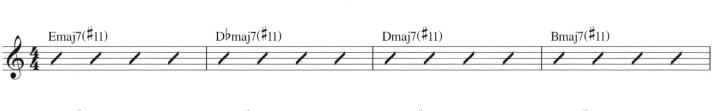

FIG. 26.3. Constant Structure Composed of Major Seventh Chords

Notice the pattern created by the bass: down a minor third, up a minor second.

A beautiful example of constant structure is in the Vince Guaraldi tune "Skating."* Listen carefully to the progression in measures 5–8, and you will hear the refreshing sound of major seventh chords moving up in minor thirds.

Listen to "Hideaway," by Moonchild to hear contiguous dominants and chords in hybrid voicing.**

---

* Vince Guaraldi Trio, *A Charlie Brown Christmas,* Fantasy, 1965.
** "Hideaway" by Amber Navran, Andrea Mattson, Max Bryk, Moonchild, *Voyager,* Tru Thoughts: TRULP341, 2017.

Part III
Modal Harmony

We have now reached the outer boundaries of functional harmony. So far, we have explored basic diatonic chords in major and minor keys; discussed tonic, subdominant, and dominant functions; added a dizzying array of chromatic alterations such as secondary and substitute dominants and their related II chords, resolving both as expected and deceptively. We invited modal interchange chords, extended and contiguous dominant patterns, and passing diminished chords to our progressions. We looked at the chord scales associated with each category of chords, then added alternative chord scales that invite yet more notes outside of the key. We even explored ways to change keys completely, all in the name of finding new ways to keep forward momentum, to keep things fresh, new, and exciting. In this last section, we will put all that aside and take a completely new approach to organizing the musical elements we are already familiar with.

Modal music presents a different harmonic paradigm—one that no longer relies on the dominant resolution as a driving force in a chord progression, but one that offers a different way of telling a story, an alternative approach to comping, improvising, and composing. While still tonal—rooted in a single tonal center—modal music is no longer functional in the traditional way of tonic, subdominant, and dominant chords. Historically, it predates functional harmony and can be traced back to the church music of the middle ages, as well as found in folk traditions around the world. Composers of the late 19th and early 20th centuries turned back to the modal tradition as a refreshing departure from functional harmony, or as an homage to folk music, which was becoming more and more influential in classical composition. Pop and rock styles of the mid 20th century, as well as many contemporary film scores, were predictably swept up by that trend as well. In jazz, a modal system of organizing harmony and improvisation came as a response to the ever faster, more complicated language of bebop, as well as the increasing exposure to music from India, Spain, and the Middle East.

In the remainder of this book, we will explore the differences between functional and modal harmony in the context of contemporary popular styles—jazz in particular. Fluid knowledge of the seven diatonic modes is crucial here, but you will also need to shift your perspective on how to think of them in the context of this very old, and at the same time, new system of musical hierarchy.

CHAPTER 27

Basic Signifiers of Modal Music

Similar to functional harmony, modal harmony is based on a tonal center—one that starts and ends the piece, occurs often and for prolonged periods of time, and generally feels like home. The tonal center, and the I chord associated with it, belong to the mode of the piece—often one of the Greek modes, but in some instances a mode of the harmonic minor or any other combination of half and whole steps is possible. The rest of the chords in the piece are derived from the same mode, or borrowed from parallel modes as modal interchange chords.

Unlike functional harmony, the chord that contains the tritone of the scale does not resolve down a fifth or down a half step, and therefore does not have a dominant function. Instead, chords that contain the characteristic pitch of the mode are used as cadential chords, creating different patterns of bringing the tonal center back at the end of a phrase. The harmonic rhythm is much slower, sometimes sitting on the tonic chord for many measures at a time, or oscillating between the tonic chord and a cadential chord over and over, thus establishing a clear tonal center without the use of a dominant resolution.

One method of diffusing the power of the tritone is by voicing chords in fourths instead of thirds, thus spreading the distance between the two notes of the tritone; or placing a tonic drone or pedal point (see chapter 29) under the chord progression, effectively anchoring it to the mode of the piece. The distinction between chord tones and tensions is largely diffused, with chords often voiced in a way that showcases all the notes of the mode, and spotlights the characteristic pitch.

In summary, a modal tune may have the following characteristics:

- lack of dominant resolution
- slow and sparse harmonic rhythm
- extensive use of the tonic I chord
- pedal point or ostinato pattern, usually in the bass
- chords voiced in fourths, no avoid notes

Here are some examples of modal music in a variety of styles.

- **Modal jazz, Dorian.** "So What" by Miles Davis. *Kind of Blue,* Columbia Records, 1959.
- **Trip-hop, Phrygian.** "Mysterons" by Portishead. *Dummy,* Go! Beat London, 1994.
- **Alternative rock, Lydian.** "Man on the Moon" by R.E.M. *Automatic for the People,* Warner Bros., 1992.
- **Rock, Mixolydian.** "Norwegian Wood" by Lennon/McCartney. The Beatles, *Rubber Soul,* Parlophone Capital, 1965.
- **Rock, Aeolian.** "Walking on the Moon" by Sting. The Police *Regatta de Blanc,* A&M, 1979.

CHAPTER 28

Characteristic Pitch and Typical Cadences for Each of the Seven Modes

We are already familiar with the seven modes of the major scale—their overall sound and characteristic pitch. Up until now, we considered modes as a displacements of the major scale, and associated each mode with a diatonic chord of the key.

In modal music, we'll explore each mode in its own right, as the tonic of the piece, with all other chords derived from it.

DORIAN

General Quality	Characteristic Pitch	Tonic Chord	Cadential Chords	Conditional Cadential	Avoid Chord
Minor	Natural 6	Imin7 or Imin6	IImin7, bVIImaj7	IV7*	VImin7b5
In C:	A	Cmin7 or Cmin6	Dmin7, Bbmaj7	F7	Amin7b5

* You may use the IV chord as a triad. If used as IV7, take special care that you don't follow that with the bVIImaj7, which will inadvertently modulate your piece to the relative Ionian key.

138

Imin
Cmin

IV
F

FIG. 28.1. Typical Cadences in Dorian

PHRYGIAN

	General Quality	Characteristic Pitch	Tonic Chord	Cadential Chords	Conditional Cadential	Avoid Chord
	Minor	♭2	Imin7	♭IImaj7, ♭VIImin7	♭III7*	Vmin7♭5
In C:		D♭	Cmin7	D♭maj7, B♭min7	E♭7	Gmin7♭5

*You may use the ♭III7 as a sus4 to avoid the tritone. If used as ♭III7, take special care that you don't follow that with the ♭VImaj7, which will inadvertently modulate your piece to the relative Ionian key.

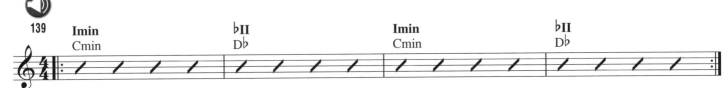

FIG. 28.2. Typical Cadences in Phrygian

LYDIAN

	General Quality	Characteristic Pitch	Tonic Chord	Cadential Chords	Conditional Cadential	Avoid Chord
	Major	#4	Imaj7	Vmaj7, VIImin7	II7*	#IVmin7♭5
In C:		F#	Cmaj7	Gmaj7, B♭min7	D7	F#7♭5

*You may use the II chord as a triad. If used as II7 take special care that you don't follow that with the Vmaj7, which will inadvertently modulate your piece to the relative Ionian key.

FIG. 28.3. Typical Cadences in Lydian

MIXOLYDIAN

General Quality	Characteristic Pitch	Tonic Chord	Cadential Chords	Conditional Cadential	Avoid Chord
Major	♭7	I7	Vmin7, ♭VIImaj7	(none)	IIImin7♭5
In C:	B♭	C7	Gmin7, B♭maj7		Emin7♭5

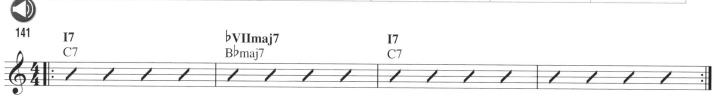

FIG. 28.4. Typical Cadences in Mixolydian

Since Ionian and Aeolian have the same makeup as major and minor respectively, we don't need to examine each chord, but do keep in mind that in order for a piece to sound in Ionian or Aeolian it should avoid having a dominant chord resolution and should include a number of the other signifiers of modal music.

Due to the unstable nature of the Imin7♭5 chord in Locrian, there are very few examples of its use in the repertoire of contemporary music.

CHAPTER 29

Pedal Point
and Ostinato

A strong signifier of modal music is the presence of a drone, pedal point, or ostinato pattern.

The practice of keeping a tonic drone underneath a melody is widespread in folk music worldwide, with certain instruments such as the bagpipe having a drone reed permanently sounding during a performance. In Indian music, we hear a shruti box sounding the root and 5th of the scale in a similar manner. The name *pedal point* originates from the organ used in church music, where the organist plays the tonic of the key using a foot pedal against the melody.

Contemporary modal music has adopted this practice, although a consistent drone is rare, and preference is now given to a rhythmic pattern underneath the chord progression. When the pattern repeats the same note and follows the rhythm of the chord progression, it is considered a pedal point and may be notated in one of two ways:

1. Slash chord symbols, where the root is to right of the chord symbol:

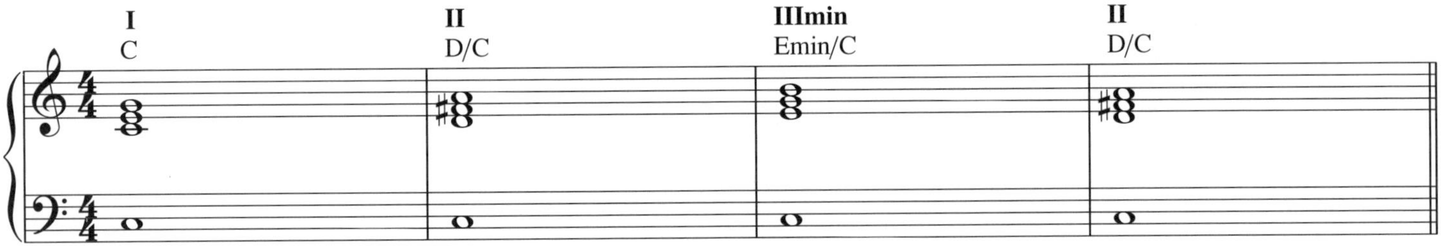

FIG. 29.1. Pedal Point Notated with Slash Chords

2. A dashed line with T.P. (tonic pedal) or D.P. (dominant pedal):

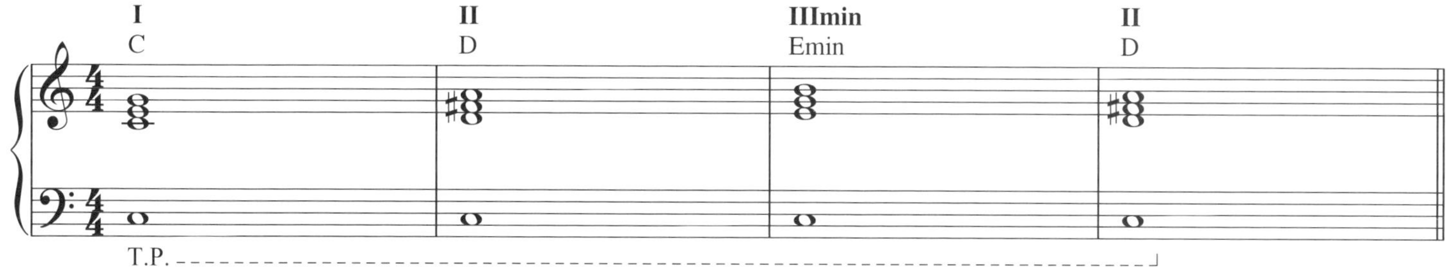

FIG. 29.2. Pedal Point Marked with T.P. or D.P.

When that rhythmic pattern is developed into a distinct rhythmic motif that repeats for an extended period of time (sometimes for the duration of the entire piece), it is called *ostinato* (derived from the Italian word for *stubborn/ obstinate*). Traditionally, an ostinato is an exact repetition of the motif. However, in contemporary music, it often conforms to the chord progression by varying in pitch to avoid undesired dissonance. The rhythm usually stays unchanged.

Some notable examples of the use of an ostinato:

*   "Boléro" by Maurice Ravel. *Boulez Conducts Ravel "Boléro,"* Sony Classical B00004T1EG, 1974.
*   "Take Five" by Dave Brubeck. The Dave Brubeck Quartet, *Time Out*, Columbia, 1959.
*   "Superstition" by Stevie Wonder. *Talking Book*, Tamla Motown, 1972.
*   "Billie Jean" by Michael Jackson. *Thriller,* Epic, 1982.
*   "Another One Bites the Dust" by John Deacon. Queen, *The Game,* EMI-Elektra, 1980.
*   "Stand By Me" by Ben E. King, Jerry Leiber, Mike Stoller. *Don't Play That Song!,* Atco, 1962.
*   "*Peter Gunn* Theme" by Henry Mancini. *The Music from Peter Gunn,* RCA Victor, 1958.
*   "Loser" by Beck, Hansen, Carl Stephenson. *Mellow Gold,* DGC Bong Load, 1994.
*   "Nardciss" by Vessela Stoyanova. *Bury Me Standing*, 2014.
*   "Prani" by Iva Bittova. *Cikori*, 2000.

ASSIGNMENT 29.1

INDEX

AABA form, 58, *60*, 60–61

ABA form, 61, *61*

accidentals
about, 4, 5, *5*
in diatonic chords, 42
notation, 5, *5*
piano and, 21–22, *21–22*
pitch change with, 22, *22*

Adele, 31

Aeolian mode
characteristics, 110, *110*, *111*
modal harmony example in, 146
polychords and, *136*

"Ain't It the Life," 93

"All I Wanna Do," 93

altered scale, 115, *115*, 117, *117*

"Another One Bites the Dust," 151

approach chords, 122, *123*

approach notes, 95–96, *96*

augmented triad, 35, *35*

avoid notes, *55*, 55–57, *56*

Babasin, Harry, 72

"Bag's Groove," 72

barline. *See* double barline; final barline; imaginary
barlines; measure line

bass
in rhythm section, *64*, 64–65, *65*
substitute dominant chords and, 98

bass clef
defined, *2*, 3
pitch and, melody, 18, *18*
treble and, overlap, 18, *18*

beam
defined, 4, *4*
groups, 22–23, *23*

the Beatles, 106, 129, 146

beats
defined, 6
hierarchy of power between, 9–10, *9–10*
notes and rests in 4/4 time and subdivision of, *7*
two-beat patterns of, 10, *10*

Beck (band), 151

"Billie Jean," 151

Bird Blues, 133, *133*

Bittova, Iva, 151

"Blackbird," 120

blues form
artists and songs for understanding, 72, 73
Bird Blues and, 133, *133*
origins of, 70, 73
phrasing and progressions, 70–73, *71*, *72*, *73*, *131*
reharmonization of, 131–33, *131–33*

"Blues in a Closet," 72

"The Blues Walk", 72

"Body and Soul," 127, 130

"Boléro," 151

Brown, Clifford, 72

Brubeck, Dave, 151

"Built for Love," 80, 102

Burke, Johnny, 93, 93*n*

cadences
of Dorian mode, 147, *147*
of Lydian mode, 148, *148*
of Mixolydian mode, 149, *149*
of Phrygian mode, 148, *148*
turnaround, *78*, 78–79, *79*
types, 51, *51*

Cason, Buzz, 129

charts, 58–61, *60*, *61*

chords. *See also* diatonic chords; diminished
chords; dominant chords; secondary dominants;
substitute dominant
cadences and, 51, *51*
chord symbols for identifying, 36
common in minor key, 90, *90*
compound minor, 89, *89*
constant structure and, 142, *142*
defined, 35
diatonic, overview, 38
dominant, overview, 49
dominant/target pairs, 77–78
harmonic function of, 50
key and, 38
major-minor, 49
modal interchange common, 94
naming conventions, 49
non-diatonic notes to progression of, 78
progressions, 43–44, *44*, 51
related II, 83, *83*
Roman numerals and symbols for, 43
root position presentation of, 44, *45*
slash, 150, *150*
V7/IV and related IImin7, 94, *94*
voice leading and, 44–45, *45*, 52–53, *53*

chord scales
    analyzing and labeling notes in, 107–8
    attached to Cmaj7, 107, *107*
    defined, 107
    diatonic chords associated with, 111, *111*
    for diatonic chords in major, 108–10, *108–10*
    for diatonic chords in minor, 112–13, *112–13*
    hybrid chord voicings by, *139*, 139–40
    for modal interchange chords, 117–18, *117–18*
    polychords by, 136, *136*
    for related II chords, 115–16, *115–16*
    for secondary dominants, 114–15, *114–15*
    for substitute dominants, 116–17, *116–17*
    symmetrical diminished scale and, 124–25, *125*
    theory, 107–18
    whole tone scale and, 115, *115*

chord voicings, 37, 45, 67–68, *68*
    hybrid, 136–40, *137–49*
    polychord, 134–36, *135*, *136*

chromatic, term defined, 42, 75

chromatic alterations, 75. *See also* secondary
   dominants; substitute dominant

chromatic scale, 24, 27, 42

circle of fifths, 39, *39*

clefs, *2*, 3. *See also* bass clef; treble clef

coda, 59, *60*, 61

"Come in with the Rain," 129

compound meters
    counting, 14
    imaginary barline in, 15, *15*
    rhythm and, 14–16, *14–16*
    simple compared with, 14
    6/8, 14–15, *15*
    triplet and, 16, *16*
    12/8, 15, *15*

compound minor chords, 89, *89*

comps, defined, 70

constant structure, 142, *142*

contiguous dominants, *141*, 141–42, *142*

Crow, Sheryl, 93

Davis, Miles, 146

Deacon, John, 151

deceptive cadence, 51, *51*

deceptive resolution
    common examples of, *105*, 105–6
    defined, 104
    to VImin chord, 104, *104*

diatonic
    harmony in minor keys, 46–47, *46–47*
    intervals, 38, 42
    passing tones, 95, *96*
    tensions on secondary dominants, 115
    term defined, 38, 42

diatonic chords
    accidentals use in, 42
    chord scales for, in major, 108–10, *108–10*
    chord scales for, in minor, 112–13, *112–13*

    overview, 38
    seventh in key of C major, *48*, 48–49
    seventh in key of C minor, 52, *52*
    seventh in natural minor, 88, *88*
    triads and, 49

diatonic triads
    D minor and major, conversion, 42, *43*
    on each degree of major scale, 42, *42*
    relative major and minor, 47, *47*

diminished chords
    ascending seventh, 120–22, *120–22*
    auxiliary, *124*, 124–25, *125*
    descending, 122–23, *123*
    enharmonic spelling of, 119, *119*
    tritones in, 119, *119*

diminished triad, 35, *35*

direct modulation, 126–27, *127*

dominant cadence, 51, *51*

dominant chords. *See also* secondary dominants;
   substitute dominant
    about, 76
    contiguous, *141*, 141–42, *142*
    deceptive resolution and, 104
    extended, *86*, 86–87, *87*
    extended substitute, 103, *103*
    finding, 77
    graphic analysis tools for, 77
    IImin7 chord relationship to, 83, *83*
    related II chord interpolated with, 87, *87*
    resolving outwards and inwards, 97, *97*
    target chord and, 77–78

dominant function
    in minor keys, 91
    secondary, 100, *120*, 120–22
    tritone interval and, 50

"Don't Know Why," 80

Dorian minor scale, 52, 90, *90*

Dorian mode, 111*n*
    characteristics, 109, *109*, 111
    chord scales for modal interchange chords and,
      117, *117*
    hybrid chords for, 139, *139*, 140
    modal harmony example in, 146
    pitch and cadences of, 147, *147*
    polychords and, *136*
    related II chords and, 116, *116*

dotted notes and rests, 9, 9–10, *10*

double barline, 4, *4*

double chromatic approach, 95, *96*

double flat, 5, *5*

double sharp, 5, *5*

drop-2 voicings, 69, *69*

drums
    basic grooves for, 63, *63*
    notation, 63, *63*
    in rhythm section, role of, 62–63
    set, 63

D.S., 59, *60*, 61

"Early Autumn," 130

eighth notes
    defined, 7, *7*
    grouping of, 8, *8*, 22–23, *23*

Ellington, Duke, 127

"Everlasting Love," 129

"Every Little Thing She Does Is Magic," 106

extended dominants, *86*, 86–87, *87*

extended substitute dominants, 103, *103*

fifths, circle of, 39, *39*

final barline, 4, *4*

"First Love Late Spring," 120

flat, 5, *5*

Foo Fighters, 93

form, term defined, 58

form reading, 58–61, *59, 60, 61*

four-way closed voicings, 68, *68*

frequency (Hz), 17

functional harmony
    modal harmony compared with modes in, 108
    modal tradition departure from, 143–44
    modes in, 108–10, *108–10*

functions, 38. *See also* dominant function;
    subdominant function
    sharp, 5

Gayden, Mac, 129

Gershwin, George and Ira, 87

grand staff
    defined, 2, *2*
    piano and, 18, *18*

Green, Johnny, 127

Guaraldi, Vince, 142, 142*n*

guitar
    in rhythm section, 65–69, *66–67, 68, 69*
    voicings for, 69, *69*

half cadence, 51, *51*

half notes, 7, *7*

harmonic function, 28

harmonic intervals, 24

harmonic minor scale, 52, 90, *90*, 91

Harrison, George, 106

H.E.R. (band), 120

"Here Comes the Sun," 106

"Here's That Rainy Day," 93, 93*n*

Herman, Woody, 130

Heyman, Edward, 130

"Hideaway," 142, 142*n*

Hill, Faith, 127, 127*n*

hybrid chord voicings
    about, 136
    in C Dorian, 139, *139*, 140
    by chord scale, chart, *139*, 139–40
    in C Ionian, 138, *138*
    in C Lydian, 138, *138*, 140
    for C Mixolydian, 139, *139*, 140
    inversion contrasted with, 137, *137*

Hz. *See* frequency

"I Got Rhythm," 87

imaginary barlines
    beat 3 visible and, 13, *13*
    in compound meters, 15, *15*
    defined, 11
    examples of, *12–15*
    exceptions and variations, 13
    sixteenth notes and, 14, *14*
    in time signature of 4/4 rewritten as 2/4, 12, *12*
    in 2/4 and 3/4 meters, 14, *14*

intervals
    descending, 33, *33*
    diatonic, 38, 42
    from Do, 32, *32*
    harmonic and melodic, defined, 24
    inversion, 33–34, *33–34*
    melodic, defined, 24
    notation, 26, *26*
    piano white note, in key of C, 34, *34*
    quality/sizes of, 24–25, *25*
    quantity and quality breakdown up to octave,
        26, *26*
    quantity as measure of, 24
    represented in major scales, 32, *32*
    represented in minor scales, 32–33, *33*
    semitones and, 24, 26
    staff and, 24
    tritone, 25, 50

inversions
    hybrid chords contrasted with, 137, *137*
    triad, 36, *36*

Ionian mode
    characteristics, 108, *108, 111*, 149
    hybrid chords for, 138, *138*
    modal music and, 149
    polychords using, 135, *135, 136*

Jackson, Michael, 151

Jackson, Milt, 72

jazz
    blues reharmonization relation to, 133, *133*
    cadence, 51, *51*

Jobim, Antônio Carlos, 102

Joel, Billy, 93, 127

Jones, Norah, 80

Jordan, Duke, 87

"Jordu," 87

keyboard. *See* piano

keys. *See also* major keys and scales; minor keys and scales
    chords and, 38
    circle of fifths and, 39, *39*
    defined, 38
    diatonic notes of, 38
    enharmonic, 39
    melody and pitch relationship with, 41, *41*
    parallel, 92
    relative, 41
    transitional modulation and, 129
    triads diatonic to, of A minor, 46, *46*

key signature
    accidentals and use of, 22
    defined, 4, *4*, 38
    format for writing, 40, *40*
    relative keys sharing same, 41
    secondary dominants and, 81

King, Ben E., 151

"Kodachrome," 129

"Lately," 80, 93

lead sheets, 59–61, *60*, *61*

ledger line
    additional, using, 20–21, *21*
    defined, 2, 3
    8va and 8vb sign compared with, 21, *21*

Lennon, John, 120, 146

Locrian mode
    characteristics, 110, *110*, *111*
    related II chords and, 115

"Loser," 151

Lydian mode
    characteristics, 109, *109*, *111*
    chord scales for modal interchange chords and, 117–18, *117–18*
    chord scales for substitute dominants and, 116–17, *116–17*
    hybrid chords for, 137, *138*, 140
    modal harmony example in, 146
    pitch and cadences of, 148, *148*
    polychords using, 135, *135*, *136*

major keys and scales
    C, written in thirds, 54
    descending, song example of, 28
    diatonic seventh chords in C major, *48*, 48–49
    diminished chords and, 119
    G and F, 28, *28*
    intervals represented in, 32, *32*
    IVmin7 used in, 92, *92*
    minor scales overlapping with, 30, *30*
    piano keyboard and, 27, *27*
    relative minor compared with, 46–47, *47*
    substitute dominants and, 98
    triads and, 35, *35*, 37, *37*, *42*, 42–43, *43*

Mancini, Henry, 151

"Man on the Moon," 146

McCartney, Paul, 120, 146

measure line (barline). *See also* imaginary barlines
    defined, *2*, 3
    double barline, 4, *4*
    final barline, 4, *4*

melodic development, 95–96

melodic intervals, defined, 24

melodic minor scale, 52, 90, *90*

melody
    pitch and key relationship with, 41, *41*
    pitch treble and bass clefs relation to, 18, *18*

Mercer, Johnny, 130

meter. *See also* compound meters
    beat emphasis and, 10, *10*
    beat hierarchy in 4/4, 9, *9*
    compound compared to simple, 14
    defined, 6

minor keys and scales. *See also* harmonic minor scale; melodic minor scale; natural minor scale
    blue note in pentatonic, 73, *73*
    blues in, 72, *72*
    common chords in, 90, *90*
    compound, 89, *89*
    diatonic chords in, 112–13, *112–13*
    diatonic harmony in, 46–47, *46–47*, 52, *52*
    dominant function in, 91
    Dorian, 52, 90, *90*
    harmonic, 52, 90, *90*, 91
    intervals represented in, 32–33, *33*
    major scales overlapping, 30, *30*
    melodic, 52
    natural, 29
    "natural minor scale" term compared with, 29
    piano keyboard and, 30, *30*
    relative major compared with, 46–47, *47*
    subV7/II in, 102, *102*
    triads and, 35, *35*, 42, *43*, 46, *46*
    variations of, 52, 88, *88*

Mitski (artist), 120

Mixolydian mode
    ascending diminished chords and, 121, *122*
    characteristics, 109, *109*, *111*
    chord scales for modal interchange chords and, 117, *117*
    chord scales for secondary dominants and, 114, *114*
    hybrid chords for, 139, *139*, 140
    modal harmony example in, 146
    pitch and cadences of, 149, *149*
    polychords using, 135, *135*, *136*

modal harmony
    characteristics and examples of, 145–46
    functional harmony relation to, 143–44
    modes compared with, 108
    pedal point and, *150*, 150–51, *151*

modal interchange
    chord scales for, 117–18, *117–18*
    chords common for, 94
    defined, 92
    function and use of, 92–93

modes. *See also specific modes*
in functional harmony, 108-10, *108-10*
in modal harmony, 147-49, *147-49*
modal harmony compared with, 108

modulation
direct, 126-27, *127*
pivot, 127-29, *128*
transitional, 129-30, *130*

Moonchild (artist), 142, 142*n*

Morton, PJ, 80, 102

"Music Box," 29, 93

"My Girl," 31

"Mysterons," 146

"Nardciss," 151

natural (notation type), 5, *5*

natural minor scale
common chords in, 90, *90*
creating, 29, *29*
degrees, 30
diatonic seventh chords in, 88, *88*
diatonic triads of A, 46, *46*
diatonic V chord in, 52, *52*
intervals of C, 33, *33*
"minor scale" term compared with, 29

neighbor tones, 95, *96*

"New York State of Mind," 93, 127

"Norwegian Wood," 146

notation and terms
basics, *2*, 2-5, *4*
chord symbols, 36
drums and, 63, *63*
intervals, 26, *26*
solid and dotted brackets and arrows, 100

note flag, 4, *4*

note head, 2, *2*
stem relationship with, 3

notes
analyzing and labeling, in chord scale, 107-8
approach, 95-96, *96*
avoid, *55*, 55-57, *56*
beaming groups of, 22-23, *23*
blue, and minor pentatonic scales, 73, *73*
chords and chord symbols for, 35-36
diatonic, of keys, 38
dotted, and rests, *9*, 9-10, *10*
dotted, ties and, 9, *9*
duration and spacing, 11, *11*
enharmonically spelled, to piano keyboard, 21, *21*
half, 7, *7*
notation and duration of, 7, *7*
piano white, intervals, 34, *34*
quarter, 7, *7*
rhythmic value of, 7, *7*, *8*
shape and rest duration, 3, *3*
sixteenth, grouping of, 8, *8*, 22-23, *23*
sixteenth, imaginary barlines and, 14, *14*
subdivision of beats and, *7*

triad, name and role, 35
voicing of chord, 37, 45, 67-68, *68*
whole, 7, *7*

note stem, 2, *2*

"Nothing Compares to You," 106

O'Connor, Sinéad, 106

"One Note Samba," 102

open voicing, 69, *69*

ostinato, 151

Parker, Charlie, 133

passing chords, 122, *123*

passing tones, 95, *96*

pedal point, *150*, 150-51, *151*

pentatonic scales
blue note and minor, 73, *73*
major, 31, *31*
major and minor, relatives, 32
minor, 31, *31*

"*Peter Gunn* Theme," 151

Pettiford, Oscar, 72

phase structures, 58-59, *59*

Phrygian mode
characteristics, 109, *109*, *111*
modal harmony example in, 146
pitch and cadences of, 148, *148*
related II chords and, 116, *116*

piano
accidentals and, 21-22, *21-22*
enharmonically spelled notes to keyboard of, 21, *21*
keyboard overview, 19, *19*
keyboard to staff position connection for, 20, *20*
ledger lines compared with 8va and 8vb sign for, 21, *21*
minor scale and keyboard of, 30, *30*
scales and keyboard of, *27*, 27-28
voicings for, 67-68, *68*
white note intervals in key of C, 34, *34*

pin, in rhythm section, 65-69, *66-67*, *68*, *69*

pitch
accidentals and change of, 22, *22*
bass clef melody and, 18, *18*
defined, 17
frequency compared with, 17
melody and key relationship with, 41, *41*
notating, 17-18, *18*
treble clef melody and, 18, *18*

pivot modulation, 127-29, *128*

Police (band), 106, 146

polychords, 134-36, *135*, *136*

Portishead, 146

"Prani," 151

"Prelude to a Kiss," 127

Pythagoras, 39

quarter notes, 7, *7*

Queen (band), 151

quick-change blues, 71, *71*

Ravel, Maurice, 151

related II chords, *83*, 83–84
    chord scales for, 115–16, *115–16*
    extended dominants and, 87, *87*

R.E.M (band), 146

repeats, 59, *60*, 61

rests
    dotted notes and, in rhythm, *9*, 9–10, *10*
    subdivision of beats and, *7*
    whole, 7, *7*

rhythm
    compound meters and, 14–16, *14–16*
    defined, 6
    dotted notes and rests in, *9*, 9–10, *10*
    grid, 11, *11*
    imaginary barlines and, 11–14, *12–14*
    one-beat and two-beat, 10, *10*
    value of notes and, 7, *7*, *8*

rhythm section
    bass in, *64*, 64–65, *65*
    drums in, 62–63, *63*
    guitar and keyboard in, 65–69, *66–67*, *68*, *69*

"Rolling in the Deep," 31

Roman numerals, chord symbols and, 43, 46, 79

scale degree
    about, 27, *27*
    Roman numerals indicating, 46

scales. *See also* major keys and scales; minor keys
  and scales
    defined, 27
    natural minor, 29, *29*
    overlapping major and minor, 30, *30*
    parallel, 29, 38
    pentatonic, 31–32, *32*
    piano keyboard and, *27*, 27–28
    relative, 38
    solfège and, 27, *27*

secondary dominants
    ascending diminished chords and, 121, *121*
    in blues reharmonization, 132, *132*
    chord scales for, 114–15, *114–15*
    creation of, *78*, 78–79, *79*
    defined, 79
    function, 80, 100, *120*, 120–22
    recognizing, 81–82
    related II chords and, 83, *83*, 84
    resolving down a fifth, 85, *85*
    tensions on, 81–82, *82*
    V7/V resolving with, 85–86

semitones, intervals and, 24, 26

seventh chords
    diatonic, in key of C major, *48*, 48–49
    diatonic, in key of C minor, 52, *52*
    voice leading, 52–53, *53*

sharp, 5, *5*

shell voicings, 68, *68*

Simon, Paul, 129

"Sir Duke," 93

sixteenth notes
    grouping of, 8, *8*, 22–23, *23*
    imaginary barlines and, 14, *14*

"Skating," 142, 142*n*

slash chords, 150, *150*

"So What," 146

Spektor, Regina, 29, 93

staff/staves. *See also* grand staff
    defined, 2, *2*
    intervals and, 24

"Stand By Me," 151

stem, 3, *3*

Stevie Wonder. *See* Wonder, Stevie

"Still on My Brain," 102

Sting (artist), 106, 146

Stoyanova, Vessela, 151

structure, constant, 142, *142*

subdominant cadence, 51, *51*

subdominant function, 50, 91
    modal interchange chords and, 93

substitute dominant (subV7)
    defined, 98
    dominant chords contrasted with, 98
    examples of using, 99, *99*
    extended, pattern, 103, *103*
    major key potential, 98
    pivot modulation and, *128*, 128–29
    related II chords and, 99, 99–102, *100*, *101*
    subV7/II and, 100
    subV7/III and, 100, *101*
    subV7/II in minor key and, 102, *102*
    subV7/IV and, 101, *101*
    subV7/V and, 101, *101*
    subV7/VI and, 102, *102*
    tritone substitution and, 97–98, *98*

substitute dominants
    bass and, 98
    chord scales for, 116–17, *116–17*
    extended, 103, *103*

subV7. *See* substitute dominant

"Superstition," 151

Swift, Taylor, 129

symmetrical diminished scale, 124–25, *125*

symmetrical dominant scale, 115, *115*

"Take Five," 151

target chord, dominant chords and, 77–78

tempo
    defined, 6
    marking, 4, *4*

the Temptations, 31

tensions
   available, *55*, 55–57, *56*
   building, 54
   chord scales and, 115, *115*
   extended dominants with, 86, *86*
   on secondary dominants, 81–82, *82*, 115
   sharp or flat notation for, 57
   substitution, in voice leading, 57, *57*
   13, avoiding, 56*n*

terms. *See* notation and terms

"They Won't Go When I Go," 87

32-bar structure, 58, *60*, 60–61

three-way closed voicings, 68, *68*

ties, 9, *9*

Timberlake, Justin, 102

time signatures
   3/2, 6
   4/4, 6, *7*
   compound meters relation to, 14–15, *15*
   defined, 4, *4*
   imaginary barlines in 4/4 rewritten as 2/4, 12, *12*

tones
   approach notes and, 95–96, *96*
   twelve tone equal temperament and, 24
   whole tone scale and, 115, *115*

tone tendencies, 28–29, 50

tonic function, 50, 91

transitional modulation, 129–30, *130*

treble clef
   bass and, overlap, 18, *18*
   defined, *2*, 3
   pitch and, melody, 18, *18*

triadic voicings, 69, *69*

triads
   diatonic seventh chords and, 49
   diatonic to key of A minor, 46, *46*
   D minor and major, *43*
   F major, with root in bass, 37, *37*
   inversions, *36*, 36–37
   major, 35, *35*, 37, *37*, *42*, 42–43, *43*
   minor, 35, *35*, 42, *43*, 46, *46*
   notes name and role in, 35
   qualities of, 35
   relative minor and major, compared, 46–47, *47*

tritones
   in diminished chords, 119, *119*
   dominant function and interval of, 50
   intervals and, 25, 50
   resolutions, 77, *77*
   substitution, 97–98, *98*
   symmetry and potential resolutions, 97, *97*

turnaround blues progression, 72, *72*

twelve tone equal temperament, 24

Van Heusen, Jimmy, 93, 93*n*

voice leading
   of chords, 44–45, *45*
   seventh chords, 52–53, *53*
   tension substitution in, 57, *57*

voicings
   of chord notes, 37, 45, 67–68, *68*
   drop-2, 69, *69*
   four-way closed, 68, *68*
   for guitar, 69, *69*
   open, 69, *69*
   for piano, 67–68, *68*
   shell, 68, *68*
   three-way closed, 68, *68*
   triadic, 69, *69*

"Walking on the Moon," 146

"The Way You Love Me," 127, 127*n*

whole notes, 7, *7*

whole rest, 7, *7*

whole tone scale, 115, *115*

Wonder, Stevie, 80, 87, 93, 127, 128, 130, 151

Wright, Yvonne, 87

"Wrong Places," 120

"You Are the Sunshine of My Life," 127, 128, 130

"You're Gonna Lose That Girl," 129

ABOUT THE AUTHORS

VESSELA STOYANOVA

Photo by nate greenslit

A widely respected performer, composer, and educator, Vessela Stoyanova melds folk music influences from her native Bulgaria, a background in classical marimba, and extensive experience with contemporary styles ranging from tango to progressive metal.

Vessela is an associate professor of harmony and jazz composition at Berklee College of Music, where she is also the assistant director for Aspire: Five-Week Summer Performance Intensive at Berklee—an influential program for young musicians that inspired the writing of this very book.

JEFF PERRY

Photo by Andy Knapp

Jeff Perry is professor of Contemporary Writing and Production at Berklee College of Music where he is also the associate director of the Aspire summer program. Jeff's professional career has spanned over forty years with performances on trumpet and electric bass throughout New England in jazz and blues, in bands as a sideman and as a leader. He has taught at Berklee College of Music since 1997 and has released four CDs of original compositions as a leader with his most recent, *Quartet*, featuring jazz standards as well. His arrangements for big band, small group jazz, and pop/rock groups have been performed throughout the U.S. He is currently residing in Swampscott, MA.